ARNE
SLOT

NOTES ON A
SEASON

ARNE
SLOT

NOTES ON A SEASON

Reach Sport
www.reachsport.com

L.F.C.

First published in Great Britain in 2025 by
Reach Sport, 5 St Paul's Square, Liverpool, L3 9SJ.

www.reachsport.com
@reach_sport

Reach Sport is a part of Reach plc.
One Canada Square, Canary Wharf, London, E15 5AP.

ISBN: 978-1-916811-49-2

Compiled by: Roy Gilfoyle, Lawrence Matheson
Artwork by: Colin Sumpter

Printed and bound by CPI Group (UK) Ltd,
Croydon, CR0 4YY.

NOTES ON A
SEASON

2024-25

"I WILL DO EVERYTHING WITHIN MY POWER TO LEAD THE TEAM IN THE BEST POSSIBLE WAY"

How do you follow a bona fide legend? That's the question Arne Slot had to answer for himself when he agreed to take over from Jürgen Klopp in the summer of 2024.

The German had spent nearly nine years turning doubters to believers as the Reds were transformed into a heavy metal, trophy-winning machine – but when the energy tank started to run low, he bowed out in the most extraordinary way possible by singing the name of the incoming head coach on the Anfield pitch in front of an emotional crowd that were still coming to terms with Klopp's departure.

How would the new man summon up the belief to walk into his new club – a daunting task at the best of times – and try to make his own mark? It must have been like going on stage after The Beatles.

To Slot's credit, he never shied away from questions about the man he was replacing and approached the task with the air of a man who was respectful of what had gone before, but supremely confident he could pick up the baton and create his own legacy.

The Dutchman knew many of the tools were there already to create a successful team. Rather than replace all the key cogs in the machine, he believed he just had to make a few tweaks here and there. And while the Reds had won the biggest prizes in the game during Klopp's reign, the only major trophy collected in the previous two seasons was the League Cup.

Slot's first big interview after becoming Liverpool head coach reflected his acknowledgement of the riches he would now have to work with, but his determination to add his own ingredients to the recipe.

"A real good team, real good players, managed to be on top for a very long time," he said when asked if the team could have a strong 2024/25 season, "but I think in the end we would all love to see Liverpool a bit higher than third place and this is the challenge we are facing now – to build on from what we have.

"I have all the confidence in this because of the players, that we can add a few things where we hopefully can get a bit more points than 82, which is necessary with the likes of Arsenal and City, to end up hopefully a bit higher than we did this season."

And so Slot used the summer weeks to implement his own ideas as quickly as he could, though there was minimal flux in the playing squad with Federico Chiesa the only addition.

By the time the first game of the season came around – a tricky-looking away day at Ipswich Town – the fans watched for clues as to what would be different under the new leader. They saw a bold half-time substitution which seemed to have the desired effect as the new era began with a 2-0 victory. Arne Slot's tenure as Liverpool head coach was up and running.

A comprehensive defeat of Manchester United on their own patch was another early test passed with flying colours and by the time Christmas arrived, the only serious blot on the Reds' copybook came via a 1-0 loss to Nottingham Forest, who themselves went on to have a successful campaign.

As Liverpool fans tucked in to their Christmas dinner, they could reflect on a four-point lead at the top of the Premier League table, a position at the summit of the new Champions League 36-team group – and look forward to a League Cup semi-final.

Slot's attention to detail and shrewd use of substitutes had resulted in a relentless consistency that made them hard to beat, even when the games were coming thick and fast.

While the European adventure was curtailed by eventual champions Paris Saint-Germain, no other team pushed Luis Enrique's men harder in the knockout phase.

The League Cup run ended in the Wembley final against Newcastle United and a bad day at the office saw an early exit in the FA Cup at Plymouth Argyle, but cup encounters failed to distract from a ruthless league campaign where it would take until April for Liverpool to lose their second game of the season.

By that time the Reds had stretched their lead at the top of the Premier League table to the point where most observers were wondering when they would clinch the title, rather than if.

Along the way they beat champions Manchester

City home and away, and claimed statement wins at Tottenham Hotspur (6-3) and West Ham (5-0), and by late April – when Spurs visited Anfield – the Reds needed one more point to guarantee they would be champions.

Despite going 1-0 down, Slot's men were in full control and, lifted by a crowd that had turned up to enjoy a party, they hit back with five goals of their own. Mo Salah – who had produced another season of countless golden moments – even had time to take a selfie with the crowd after scoring his own inevitable goal.

"The only moment I was emotional today was when we arrived at the stadium – to see what it meant for the fans, what it meant for these people," explained the man who had helped Feyenoord to become Eredivisie champions in 2023. "For us to have a chance of winning it felt really special but immediately it also felt like, 'We still have to do it.' But I think everybody who was inside that bus felt that if the fans are with us, like they are, then it's impossible for us to lose this game of football. During the game, after the game, it's been incredible how the support of the fans was and how our players played. Special to be part of this day."

With four games to go, the Reds had reached 82 points, the total Slot had mentioned had been earned in the 23/24 campaign. A few adjustments here and there had propelled Liverpool to the mark with 12 still left to play for.

With the job already done, the new champions would claim only two of those points, yet enjoy a guard of honour four times – and the fans would introduce a new song that claimed 'he brought us number 20 and his name is Arne Slot'.

Slot had been right when he said we would all love to see Liverpool a bit higher than third and when Virgil van Dijk raised the Premier League trophy in front of a packed Anfield – a fan-centric experience Klopp had never been able to enjoy as the COVID pandemic impacted the 2019/20 celebration – the new boss could see how much it meant to everyone for the Reds to be at the top of English football for the 20th time.

This book is a reminder of that incredible journey, lived through Slot's official matchday programme notes, from his maiden home game in charge against Brentford, through to the special edition against Crystal Palace on the day Liverpool completed a brilliant season.

With facts, statistics and post-match reactions from every one of the 56 games, it's a journey every Liverpool supporter will be happy to relive.

It was a journey made possible by a man who knew what he had inherited and had the confidence to know how to squeeze even more out of a squad and a club that was already in a good place, but could get to an even better place.

In his own understated way, the final word should go

to the man who led the charge in 2024/25, becoming the first Dutchman to coach a team to the Premier League title, these words again taken from the interview he conducted immediately after arriving at Liverpool.

"There is a change but the change hopefully isn't that big, because we still have the same players, we still have the same fans – and if the both of them are going to do the same job, that will make my life a lot more easy! I'm expecting them to show up again in the upcoming season, and the same for the players. I will do everything within my power to lead the team in the best possible way."

L.F.C.

AUG

2024

The departure of a club icon and a quiet
summer in the transfer market meant
all eyes were on the dugout as fans and
interested onlookers wondered how
the club would react in the immediate
post-Klopp era with a tricky-looking trip
to a newly-promoted side the first test
for Arne Slot's new-look setup

Coming up:
17th: Ipswich Town (PL) A
25th: Brentford (PL) H

Saturday, August 17th, 12.30pm
Premier League
Ipswich Town 0 Liverpool 2

Goals: Jota (60), Salah (65)

Line-up (4-2-3-1): Alisson, Alexander-Arnold (Bradley 77), Quansah (Konate 46), Van Dijk (c), Robertson (Tsimikas 79), Gravenberch, Mac Allister, Salah, Szoboszlai, Diaz, Jota (Gakpo 79). Subs not used: Kelleher, Elliott, Endo, Jones, Nunez

Arne's post-match reaction: 'We as a team made a big change at half-time because we came out totally different to how we had come out in the first half. I have to give credit to Ipswich as well because I think they were aggressive; they were not afraid; they were playing one-v-one all over the pitch to defend us. Then it is about winning your duels and winning your second balls. I think they won more than us, and that's why it was absolutely an equal game in the first half. Second half, we won more duels, we won more second balls, and we played more balls in behind because if the other team takes the risk of playing one-v-one and you have the likes of Luis Diaz, Mo Salah, and Diogo Jota, then use them, play the balls in behind. That's what we did better in the second half, and from there on gaps opened up, and you could see how well we could play in possession.

They were very aggressive, which led to three yellow cards – but in a good way aggressive – and we didn't cope with that well *enough, in my opinion. That's what I said to them at half-time, if you want to win here, then you need to go a step up in terms of winning your duels first and make a fight out of it, instead of accepting that every time we play a ball long, the ball ends up in our 16 again.*

For me, it is always about the team, so if individual performance is really good, that is because the team does really well. Everybody is emphasising on the goal Mo scored and the assist he had, but both goals were from a build-up situation where we started one time with Virgil [van Dijk] and the other time, I think, even with Alisson [Becker]. So, we need to make sure these players, the attackers, come into promising positions, and the team needs to help them with that.

When I started here, there were many things that had been told to me, but one of them was that Jürgen [Klopp] hated the 12.30 kick-off, and today the team showed that we hated the 12.30 kick-off because we were not in the game in the first half. And the second thing people told me is that there are no easy games in the Premier League, and we showed that today. If you play against a newly promoted team and they can make such a fight out of it as they did in the first half, they can make it so difficult for us, then there's probably a lot more to come.'

Post-match notes

Mo Salah has now scored more goals (nine) than anyone else on the first day of a Premier League season.

v Brentford
Sunday, August 25th, 4.30pm

'ONE OF THE BEST THINGS ABOUT TODAY IS THAT WE GET TO SHARE THE EXCITEMENT TOGETHER'

Premier League

Good afternoon and welcome to our first home Premier League game of the season against Brentford.

I know from past experience as a football fan, as a player and a coach that this will be a special day for many people. It is a moment that all of us look forward to because it brings so many possibilities and opportunities, and one of the best things about today is that we get to share this excitement together.

I do not want to dwell too much on the fact that this will be my first competitive fixture at Anfield in my new role as head coach. It goes without saying that this is a big honour for me and also for my staff, but at the same time our only focus will be on the game itself, not on any personal feelings or side issues.

Having said that, it is important that I say thank you to everyone who has made my staff and myself so welcome from the moment we came here. Before I arrived I was told that Liverpool is a family club, and it has definitely lived up to this description in so many ways. This is something that we are very grateful for.

In this spirit, I would like to say welcome to every single supporter who is at today's game. Whether it is your first game or the latest of hundreds, I hope it is as enjoyable an experience as you hope for. Welcome also to Thomas Frank and his staff.

Brentford are a club who have a very good reputation in this country and in Europe also because of what they have achieved in the Premier League in recent seasons.

This means they will be a big challenge for us, so we have to be ready for that. The positive is that we go into the match with three points on the board already. We wanted a good start against Ipswich Town last weekend, and after a difficult first half against a tricky and determined opponent, we got one.

As with almost every game, there were things I liked a lot and elements that I was not so happy with. This is totally normal, of course, especially at the very start of a new season, and this is why the hard work continues on the training ground so that we can look to improve the parts that worked well and the parts that did not work quite so well.

I have said a few times that my responsibility is always to look for perfection even though we all know that perfection is not really achievable. It is about being the very best that we can be, as individuals and as a team, and part of this process is never falling into the trap of thinking we are good enough or that we have done enough.

As I have said many times since coming here, I inherited a very good team from Jürgen, and our responsibility now is to do everything we can to build on this legacy. We have a lot of quality, and there is also a really positive culture in place so that the opportunity for us to improve is clear even though it is just as clear that the team did really well last season.

We are now just taking the first steps in that journey,

and if our experience of football should tell us anything, it is that it will not be easy. But this is also what makes it so exciting. When a club like this one goes in a different direction or looks to become even stronger than it already is, it does so in the knowledge of what is possible and also the support that we will have along the way.

This support is not something we take for granted, though. We know it constantly has to be earned, and that the only way to do this is by giving absolutely everything we have on and off the pitch. Today is about making good on our side of this bargain, so hopefully we can do that.

Liverpool 2 Brentford 0

Goals: Diaz (13), Salah (70)

Line-up (4-2-3-1): Alisson, Alexander-Arnold (Bradley 73), Konate, Van Dijk (c), Robertson, Gravenberch (Endo 90+1), Mac Allister, Salah (Elliott 83), Szoboszlai, Diaz (Gakpo 72), Jota (Nunez 72). Subs not used: Kelleher, Gomez, Quansah, Tsimikas

Arne's post-match reaction: 'Positive for many reasons. I think Brentford showed last week with their first goal, but in general also in their first game, that they can play out from the back really good. They tried to do this here as well; sometimes it worked better than other moments, but they are also really threatening on the counter-attack, and they are obviously a big threat on set-pieces, and I think the only threat they had today was the set-piece where Alisson [Becker] saved us in the second half. It was also pleasing to see that from their set-piece we could score our first goal.

It's nice to inherit a team and individuals that are so special, and that's what you saw in the first goal as well. I think Lucho [Diaz] finished it off really well. Mo [Salah] won an important duel around the 18-yard box – because this is what the margins in football are; if he would have lost that duel, they would have maybe got a shot on target. He won the duel, and then we could counter-attack them, and Diogo [Jota] made a great pass with the right timing and a great run, and he finished it off really well.

The reception of the fans was similar to the reception I got from all the people in and around the AXA [Training Centre] and the people who are working for Liverpool. So, I think I cannot speak for all of the managers, but I think maybe all of them would tell you the same: every manager that comes in here feels the warmth of this club, feels the appreciation of the fans, and the most important thing we have to do as managers is to make sure the team plays in a style that the fans like to see.'

Post-match notes

Luis Diaz scored on his 100th appearance for the club on what was Arne Slot's first home match in charge. Brentford have lost all four of their Premier League games at Anfield by an aggregate score of 9-0.

SEP

2024

An unexpected home defeat
tempers optimism during an
otherwise faultless month that
saw cup adventures begin and
a comprehensive humbling of
long-standing rivals in their
own back yard

Coming up:
1st: Manchester United (PL) A
14th: Nottingham Forest (PL) H
17th: Milan (CL) A
21st: Bournemouth (PL) H
25th: West Ham United (CC) H
28th: Wolverhampton Wanderers (PL) A

Sunday, September 1st, 4pm
Premier League
Manchester United 0 Liverpool 3

Goals: Diaz (35, 42), Salah (56)

Line-up (4-2-3-1): Alisson, Alexander-Arnold (Bradley 76), Konate, Van Dijk (c), Robertson (Tsimikas 83), Gravenberch, Mac Allister, Salah, Szoboszlai, Diaz (Gakpo 66), Jota (Nunez 76). Subs not used: Kelleher, Quansah, Elliott, Endo, Gomez

Arne's post-match reaction: 'I don't [think the game could have been any better for Liverpool]. I think everything you want to see as a manager you saw in this game. So, there were difficult moments for us – I think United started really well, and we conceded one or two corner kicks in that moment. But we fought ourselves through those moments, and then we got the disallowed goal, but there was no negative reaction at all; we just kept on playing afterwards, scoring three. We could have scored more, two important saves from Ali [Becker] in the second half. So, everything was there, and maybe the one that was most important is that the work rate was incredible by all of them without the ball, and that makes it a very positive day today.

I normally don't use the word 'proud,' but what I think we did very well in all three games is, like I just mentioned, the work rate without the ball. So, we try to press the opponent as high as we can but if they play through or over our press, I see everybody *working really hard to make sure we don't need Ali and sometimes we do and then it's a good thing that we have a real good goalkeeper. What impressed me most today was the way we played with the ball because I know what we can do without the ball, but the way we played with the ball was, I think, also very good today.*

It was special to be involved in this game, and it's only special if you win it, and that's what we did. So, [I am] really pleased that we won it but maybe even more with the game and how we did it today.

When we had ball possession, we were hoping that we could find one of our midfielders open or free every time. But, again, also these three played a very good game, but they need their centre-backs to play the ball through the lines. They need the centre-backs to be close to them for the moments they cannot arrive, then Ibou [Konate] was there, Virgil [van Dijk] was there... Virgil every time stepped into the midfield defensively, also. Like I said, it was a team performance, and, you know me a bit now, it is always about the team, and then the individual can show himself. I think all 11 of them and the ones that came in played a very good game.'

Post-match notes

Mo Salah has scored (11) or assisted (six) 17 of Liverpool's last 26 goals against Manchester United.

Arne Slot

**v Nottingham Forest
Saturday, September 14th, 3pm**

'OUR FOOTBALL HAS BEEN GOOD AND THE REWARDS WE HAVE HAD HAVE BEEN DESERVED'

Premier League

Good afternoon and welcome to Anfield for our Premier League fixture against Nottingham Forest.

This is our first game after the international break, so the target is to pick up where we left off as we enter a period of the season that we know is going to be more intense than what went before.

Up until this point, we have played one game each week, but from now on we will play a match pretty much every three days, so we have to be ready for that because the challenges will come thick and fast.

As a squad and as a staff, we have to be prepared for what is coming. Today we have the Premier League; in midweek we will play in the Champions League, then we have Premier League again, and then it is Carabao Cup. This is all within the space of eleven days, so it is a big challenge but also an exciting one.

The big positive is that we enter into this period having started the season well. Aside from the first half against Ipswich Town on the opening day, our football has been good, and the rewards we have had have been deserved.

Our early objective was to take as many points as we could from our first three games, and we managed to do that. At the same time, though, neither myself nor anyone else associated with the first team believes we have done so well that there is no room for improvement. In reality, the opposite is true.

This is not to dampen excitement or to play down expectations – we want our fans to believe in what we are doing and to have hopes based on what they are seeing from the team. But at the same time, we have a collective responsibility to find areas for improvement wherever they may be, and this will always be our approach whether results are good, bad, or indifferent.

The team had a lot of praise after our win against Manchester United, and much of it was deserved, but just as we are aware of the things we did well, we also know that there are certain elements that we could have done better. The start of the match was difficult, for example, and we also had some moments where Alisson had to make really good saves.

Again, highlighting these issues isn't to downplay the result or the performance. If we can be good – and we were certainly good at Old Trafford – but still know that we can get better, this is not a bad position to work from.

To put it as simply as I can – we have made a good start, but there is still so much to prove.

I would like to welcome Nuno Espírito Santo and the staff, players, and officials of Nottingham Forest to Anfield. Of course we are aware that Forest have made a good start to the season themselves and will come into this fixture unbeaten, so we should be prepared for the kind of challenge that a team in this kind of moment will bring.

They also won two of their final three games of last season, so it is clear that Nuno is adding a consistency to their play and also their results. Forest are hard to beat and will be hard to beat. I am sure that their ambitions for this season will be to improve on the previous one as much as possible, so for all of these reasons we should expect to face a tough opponent.

Finally, I would like to take this opportunity to pay my respects to Ron Yeats on behalf of all of the Liverpool staff and players.

I have not been at the club for too long, and I know Ron had been ill for a while, so I never had the fortune of meeting him, but from the stories I have heard and read, it is clear that he was and always will be a legendary figure in the history of Liverpool FC.

It is always a privilege to follow on from players and coaches who set the standards. It is also a responsibility that all of us take very seriously.

More than anything, though, our thoughts are with Ron's family, friends, and former team-mates.

Liverpool 0 Nottingham Forest 1

Line-up (4-2-3-1): Alisson, Alexander-Arnold, Konate (Jones 75), Van Dijk (c), Robertson (Tsimikas 75), Gravenberch, Mac Allister (Bradley 60), Salah, Szoboszlai, Diaz (Gakpo 61), Jota (Nunez 60). Subs not used: Kelleher, Quansah, Endo, Gomez

Arne's post-match reaction: 'I think the only thing we had influence on was ball possession because they played a lot of long balls, so if you then take the ball back, you need to go past

11 players. We had a lot of ball possession but only managed to create three [or] four quite good chances, so that is by far not enough if you have so much ball possession. If you play so much in their half, we need to do much better. We lost the ball so many times in simple situations. That is, I think, the main story from the game: ball possession not good enough.

I don't think it had anything to do with it [on whether the international break was a factor]. Players came back strong, and I saw today also a team that wanted to fight until the end. So it had nothing to do with energy, in my opinion, but we simply had the ball a lot, and we had to create from ball possession. If you look at the goals we have scored until now, we also scored quite a few from transition moments, from winning the ball back and then going to transition.

But it is a big setback. If you lose a home game, it's always a setback, especially if you face a team... we never know; maybe they will go all the way to fight for Champions League tickets, but normally this team is not ending up in the top 10, so if you lose a game against them, that's a big disappointment. Although, they were organised and structured really well today.'

Post-match notes

This was Nottingham Forest's first win at Anfield since 1969.

Tuesday, September 17th, 8pm
UEFA Champions League
AC Milan 1 Liverpool 3

Goals: Konate (23), Van Dijk (41), Szoboszlai (67)

Line-up (4-2-3-1): Alisson, Alexander-Arnold (Gomez 79), Konate, Van Dijk (c), Tsimikas, Gravenberch, Mac Allister (Endo 90+3), Gakpo (Diaz 68), Szoboszlai, Salah (Chiesa 90+3), Jota (Nunez 68). Subs not used: Kelleher, Jaros, Bradley, Jones, Morton, Quansah, Robertson

Arne's post-match reaction: 'Normally you celebrate your birthday with your friends and your family. But this was a real good alternative to play a first Champions League game against a special club for Liverpool, but also a special club for Dutch people in a nice venue. Then to win it the way we did after going 1-0 down after five minutes with the result of Nottingham Forest still in our head. I think it was very good to see how they took the game in their hands, the players, and in the end we scored three goals and won 3-1.

I was standing just a second ago next to Clarence Seedorf. They also talked about Ryan [Gravenberch] and Cody [Gakpo], and I said it's a special place for Dutch players to play because of the former players that have played here. To put a performance in like this is always nice as a Liverpool player, and at a venue like this, it's even nicer. Yes, you can pick these two, but I think

I could pick a few others as well that played really well. Like always, it's very difficult for an individual to play well if the whole team doesn't play well and vice versa. The whole team played well, and then the individuals can shine from there.

We were a bit disappointed with the result against Nottingham Forest, [but] we were also disappointed from getting eight corner kicks and not scoring, but we were very close. We felt with all the work we put in on set-pieces that at some moment we should get the reward.

I think [it was] two very good set-pieces and two very good headers that got us two goals, which was important because I think we were very comfortable on the ball, pressed really well, but in the end you need goals as well. We hit the crossbar a few times today out of open play, so we needed set-pieces. and it was good to see that we scored them for all the work my assistants and the players put in. It is nice to see it got rewarded today.

It sounds a bit weird if you play three, four, five minutes and we already conceded one chance, which was offside, and then afterwards you concede a goal [and] that I'm going to tell you now that we didn't even start bad.'

Post-match notes

Arne Slot became the fourth manager to win a Champions League game on his birthday following Bobby Robson, Roberto Mancini and Arsene Wenger.

v Bournemouth
Saturday, September 21st, 3pm

'RESPONDING TO A SETBACK BECOMES LESS HARD WHEN EVERYONE PULLS TOGETHER'

Premier League

Good afternoon and welcome to Anfield for our Premier League fixture against AFC Bournemouth.

Before I look ahead to today's game, I want to look back at the last one. Winning at a stadium like the San Siro against a team with the history and stature of AC Milan is something that everyone associated with Liverpool FC should be proud of.

Sometimes it can be easy to take these kind of results for granted, but we never should. For every single player, staff member, and supporter who contributed, I hope you were able to enjoy the moment because it was a special one.

For the team, the priority was to bounce back from a really disappointing result against Nottingham Forest a few days earlier. It was inevitable that we would have that defeat in our heads a little bit, especially after going a goal down so early, but the performance showed resilience, quality, and character, and this is why we were able to get an important win.

I said afterwards that the whole team played well, and the reason for this is the hard work that the players put in. Responding to a setback is one of those things that is always easier said than done, but it definitely becomes less hard when everyone pulls together with a focus on putting things right, and this is exactly what happened.

The key now is to build on what we have done so far. We cannot change the loss to Forest, but we can continue to learn from it and keep on improving.

This will be our objective again today because, just like Forest one week ago, we know full well that Bournemouth will have their own ambitions of getting a positive result at Anfield.

Of course, I would like to welcome Andoni Iraola, his staff, and the players and supporters of Bournemouth to the stadium. Bournemouth's story in recent years is one that it is very hard not to like and respect. They more than punch their weight in the Premier League and have a reputation for playing good football, which is very much deserved.

So we know what to expect, and this is another tough challenge against an opponent with quality and experience. We did not arrive back from Milan until the early hours of Wednesday morning, but by the time kick-off arrives our aim is to be ready to go again because we know another good performance will be required.

I mentioned earlier how pleased I was with the players in midweek, and the same goes for our fans. During the game itself I was totally focused on what was happening on the pitch, so it was only afterwards that I was able to fully appreciate the impact that our supporters had on the stadium.

Seeing so many of you up in the Gods, spread across an entire stand, was a wonderful thing, and the support that we received throughout the game was incredible. Even though you were so heavily outnumbered, you really made yourselves heard, and this definitely helped our performance.

We can only ever appreciate this kind of support, especially when it happens in a foreign country, meaning our fans have to travel a long way to give us their backing. This is why everyone at the club was so saddened by the tragic loss of Philip Dooley while we were in Italy.

Liverpool is a special club, and one of the main reasons for this is our supporters, so to lose one of them in circumstances like this is incredibly sad. It goes without saying that our sympathies and our thoughts are with Philip's family and friends.

Liverpool 3 Bournemouth 0

Goals: Diaz (26, 28), Nunez (37)

Line-up (4-2-3-1): Kelleher, Alexander-Arnold, Konate, Van Dijk (c), Robertson, Gravenberch, Mac Allister, Salah, Szoboszlai (Jones 61), Diaz (Gakpo 72), Nunez (Chiesa 72). Subs not used: Jaros, Bradley, Gomez, Quansah, Jota, Tsimikas

Arne's post-match reaction: 'There were 12 minutes where we scored three goals, but I think during the whole first half we saw many of those moments. Unfortunately for us, the first, second, and third didn't go in. The good thing for us was their first chance didn't go in as well. Then there were these 12 minutes of one attack after another that led to three goals, which was really pleasing to see at that moment – and which we also needed because we played against a tough opponent. An opponent which showed today that even when they were 3-0 down, they just kept on going. It was tougher than the result might look.

The finishes [Diaz's] in both situations were really good, but I think the lead-up to both goals was different, and that's why it was really good. In the first goal, Ibou [Konate] recognised that they had a high last line and they wanted to press us really high, completely different to Nottingham Forest. He recognised the right moment to play the ball in behind. In the second one, we needed to play Mo [Salah], and Trent [Alexander-Arnold] reacted fantastically by coming underneath, bounced pass [to] Mo, and he just went all the way with the ball all over the pitch and assisted Lucho. Both team goals with different set-ups.

I said to them today in the pre-match meeting that I learn from them day by day, and I was really curious to see how we would react after the Milan game. What I know from the start – and what I knew before I even started – is that there is a lot of quality in this team; that's clear, but we are not the only one. There are a lot of quality teams in this league.'

Post-match notes

Victory meant Liverpool had won 10 of their last 11 meetings with Bournemouth in a match that saw Federico Chiesa make his league debut from the bench.

**v West Ham United
Wednesday, September 25th, 8pm**

'FOR US IT IS ABOUT DOING EVERYTHING WE CAN TO REACH THE NEXT ROUND'

Carabao Cup third round

Good evening and welcome to Anfield for our Carabao Cup tie against West Ham United.

I am well aware that under Jürgen, Liverpool won this trophy in special circumstances last season and that the club has a very strong tradition in this competition.

These are the kind of elements – the moments, the history, and the glory – which makes Liverpool the club that it is, and we should always look to use them to inspire us because they show what is possible.

Tonight, though, is only the start of a journey for us as a group. Yes, the players will have muscle memory from last season, and this can help us, of course, but at the same time we know we have to take our own steps and see where they take us. We cannot depend on what happened before.

There has been a lot of focus on which team I would select for this tie, but the reality is quite simple – I will select one that I feel is in our best interests both in terms of looking to qualify for the next round and using the squad as best as we possibly can.

At the time of writing these notes, the players have not trained since the win over AFC Bournemouth, so, as usual, it will be a case of assessing who is best placed to start this game, but one thing should be very clear – whoever takes to the field will be capable of contributing to what we hope will be another strong team performance.

This is what we got against Bournemouth on Saturday,

and there were many things that pleased me about how we played and the way that we competed. The goals speak for themselves, of course, but there were many other positives that do not grab attention in the same way, and it is important that we recognise them because we will need them going forward.

One of the areas that pleased me most was our willingness to defend and our desire not to concede goals. One of the best examples was Caoimhin Kelleher, who was determined to keep a clean sheet and made some very good saves, but there were many other examples from players in all positions, whether this involved making blocks, winning duels, chasing back, or being in the right position.

Which is not to say we got everything right. The fact that Caoimhin had to make as many saves as he did shows that there were occasions when we could have defended better, but the overall commitment to defending was very pleasing to see, especially as it is a quality that we are going to need, not just tonight but in every game going forward.

Before the last game I actually told the players that I am still learning from them day by day, and one of the things I was curious about was how they would react to beating AC Milan in the Champions League. I had already seen their reaction to the defeat against Nottingham Forest, and this was very positive, but reacting to a big win against one of Europe's most historical clubs is also a test in its own way. We had faced a similar situation after beating Manchester United, and we followed that up with the loss to Forest, so it was very pleasing to see us cope with these kind of challenges the way we did over the last week because it shows a strong mentality. Again, we will need this tonight and in the future.

Finally, I would like to welcome Julen Lopetegui, his staff and players, and everyone associated with West Ham to Anfield for tonight's game. I know they will have the same desire to reach the next round as we have, so our starting point will be to respect that.

For us, it is about looking to produce another good performance and doing everything we can to reach the next round. Hopefully we can achieve these objectives.

Liverpool 5 West Ham United 1

Goals: Jota (25, 49), Salah (74), Gakpo (90, 90+3)

Line-up (4-2-3-1): Kelleher, Bradley, Gomez (c), Quansah, Tsimikas (Robertson 82), Endo (Morton 82), Jones, Chiesa (Salah 59), Jota (Mac Allister 59), Gakpo, Nunez. Subs not used: Jaros, Alexander-Arnold, Diaz, Szoboszlai, Van Dijk

Arne's post-match reaction: 'You already start to laugh because you're thinking, for two months I only ask about new players! I constantly told you guys how many quality players we already had. I think you all knew, and that's also what we showed in the last weeks, and today again, that we have many quality players.

What pleased me most was that even if a lot of new players come in, they don't come in and try to have a good individual performance. They try to work really hard for the team. There was a lot of desire not to concede, and as a result of that, we had some good individual performances as well.

I think Diogo [Jota] deserved it because he played a lot of good games for us already. If I'm correct, he was only on the scoresheet in the first game against Ipswich. He's been important for us in every single game he played, but a striker also wants to score goals. I'm pleased for him that he scored two today, although he played in a No. 10 position. He scored two really good goals, and Cody [Gakpo], I think it was 10, 15, or 20 minutes before the end where he cleared the ball in his own 18-yard box, and that is also what he brings to our game.

If I see him in training, the way he hits the ball in and around the 18-yard box is with incredible speed. So, I'm not surprised to see him scoring like this. Someone just told me he scored a similar one last season in this cup tie against West Ham. So, I'm not surprised to see him score; not in the way he did, but it's not only about them scoring, it's also about them defending.'

Post-match notes

For the second successive season the Reds beat West Ham 5-1 at home in the Carabao Cup.

Saturday, September 28th, 5.30pm
Premier League
Wolverhampton W 1 Liverpool 2

Goals: Konate (45+2), Salah (61 pen)

Line-up (4-2-3-1): Alisson, Alexander-Arnold, Konate, Van Dijk (c), Robertson (Gomez 89), Gravenberch, Mac Allister, Salah, Szoboszlai (Jones 73), Diaz (Gakpo 73), Jota. Subs not used: Kelleher, Bradley, Chiesa, Endo, Quansah, Tsimikas

Arne's post-match reaction: 'It's maybe for others to judge, but I think the first 15 minutes were difficult for us. The other team − Wolves − had a week to prepare, and if you have a very good manager like Gary O'Neil, who is tactically really strong and comes up with a strong game plan, that's what he did. We were ready for this. You always have to wait to [see] then exactly what he does. He overloaded our right side in a good manner, which made it difficult for us to control the game in the first 15 to 20 minutes. Then when it [the game] lied down a bit, the energy went away maybe, and then I think we took more control.

For me, it wasn't a surprise the moment we scored a goal because I thought that in those moments we were getting better and better. We get a big chance with Dominik Szoboszlai, and I was almost surprised that we conceded [in] the second half because I felt in the second half [that] we had much more control than in the first half. We conceded a goal that was avoidable, let's put it that way.

It's almost ideal that we played Wolves today because we are top and they're last, and they absolutely don't deserve to be last. They had a very difficult fixture list and I've seen many games of them, and in almost every game they deserve more. You could even argue [that] today because it wasn't like we were so much better than them. They were in the game [and] doing a lot of good things. If they keep doing this against other teams as well, they will never end up No. 20 [in the league]. We still have to prove that when we come across Arsenal, Newcastle, Chelsea [and] Aston Villa [to see] if we can then still be up there with Champions League games included as well.

I think everybody is realistic enough. All the players have so much experience that they understand six games into the season doesn't give you a realistic view on the league table. That is more like in 19 games, then you can really feel, 'Okay, where are we?' But of course, it helps if you get some good results, especially if you bring in a new manager and a new staff and being a successor of such a successful one. Of course everybody understands that if we'd have lost four or five out of these first six fixtures, that life would've been a bit different than it is.'

Post-match notes

A hard-fought victory at Molineux moved the Reds to the top of the Premier League table.

OCT

2024

Momentum really begins to build as an unbeaten month contained several hard-fought victories, including two in the new-look Champions League format, plus match-ups with a couple of title contenders

Coming up:
2nd: Bologna (CL) H
5th: Crystal Palace (PL) A
20th: Chelsea (PL) H
23rd: RB Leipzig (CL) A
27th: Arsenal (PL) A
30th: Brighton & Hove Albion (CC) A

v Bologna
Wednesday, October 2nd, 8pm

'NOTHING HAS EVER BEEN GIVEN TO LIVERPOOL. IT HAS ALWAYS BEEN EARNED'

Champions League group phase

Good evening and welcome to Anfield for our Champions League fixture against Bologna.

Of course I have heard a lot about European nights at Anfield, and this is my first opportunity to experience one as Liverpool head coach, so it is something that I am very much looking forward to.

We already have three points on the board thanks to our victory in Milan a couple of weeks ago, so now we have the opportunity to build on the positive start we have made, and this time the chance comes in front of our own supporters. We should do everything we can to make the most of it.

When I joined Liverpool, I knew all about the club's history in Europe – the great moments, the great games, the success, and so on – but I am also aware that everything that has been achieved has come through hard work, desire, and ability. Nothing has ever been given to Liverpool. It has always been earned.

It will be exactly the same tonight and in the weeks and months to come. The new Champions League structure is still settling, and it will only be in time that we fully understand the differences it will make, but one thing we know for sure already is that we will have to win as many games as possible against teams who have the very same objective.

Bologna clearly falls into this category. They have had a remarkable couple of years in Serie A during a period in which they established themselves as one of Europe's most exciting up-and-coming clubs. Their recent story is a really interesting one, so I would like to welcome Vincenzo Italiano, his staff and players to Anfield with warmth and respect in the knowledge that Bologna will be a tough test.

Although this will be our penultimate game before the international break, the combination of the situation we are in and the schedule we are facing means there can and will be no easing up. This is our second of three matches inside one week, and the challenges are continuing to come to us, so we need to be ready for them.

I have said from the start of the season that these are the kind of periods when we will find out a lot about where we are at. Playing Saturday-Wednesday-Saturday in two competitions is always a big challenge in so many ways. It tests our squad, our preparation, our recovery, our ability to cope with different pressures, and so many other things besides.

This isn't to say we haven't already learned a lot about ourselves from the games when we played only once a week, but it definitely makes sense that you learn more during spells like this. Part of this process involves always being realistic so that we recognise exactly where we are in our development as a team.

The results at the weekend mean we are currently on top of the Premier League, and this is something that the players should be pleased with, of course. But at the same time we know that the fixtures we have had at the start of the season have not been as hard as they have been for other teams.

This isn't about dampening excitement because we always want our supporters to believe in what we are doing and the possibilities it might bring. It is about being realistic and understanding our own progress because by doing this we can keep on obtaining the information that we need to keep on improving.

If we can keep on being serious in our approach in this way, it can only help us, especially as this is our first season back in the Champions League after missing out last time around. Staying humble, keeping our feet on the ground, and knowing there is a lot of hard work and improvement still required is not just the right way for us; it is the only way.

Hopefully tonight we can take another step in the right direction.

Liverpool 2 Bologna 0

Goals: Mac Allister (11), Salah (75)

Line-up (4-2-3-1): Alisson, Alexander-Arnold (Bradley 85), Konate, Van Dijk (c), Robertson (Tsimikas 72), Gravenberch, Mac Allister, Salah, Diaz (Gakpo 72), Szoboszlai (Jones 86), Nunez (Jota 61).
Subs not used: Jaros, Kelleher, Endo, Morton, Quansah, Nyoni, Gomez

Arne's post-match reaction: '[It was] a good one because it was a win. It wasn't an easy one, but that's normal if you play

Champions League; there is always a lot of resistance, and a lot of good teams play in the Champions League – and Bologna is one of them. You could also see the [other] results tonight, where we saw some surprising results. It was good to win, a clean sheet, and some good individual performances, so positive overall.

The thing is, you will probably never reach perfection. You are always aiming for perfection, but you will never reach this. We can improve, we have to improve, that's clear – but there are also a lot of positives to take from tonight and also from the other games. There was a spell in the game where we didn't control and they were threatening us more than I would like to see, but again, this is normal. I saw a lot of games yesterday. I saw some games before we played in the Champions League [and] it is never that only one team plays – there are always two teams playing. I think for most parts of the game we controlled, we had more ball possession, but they threatened us, especially in the last phase of the first half a few times.

What can I say about Mo [Salah]? What you saw today is what you get. If you bring him often enough in positions like this, he can score a goal. He had a great assist as well.'

Post-match notes

Mo Salah scored his 49th Champions League goal as the Reds won their second successive group phase match.

Saturday, October 5th, 3pm
Premier League
Crystal Palace 0 Liverpool 1

Goal: Jota (9)

Line-up (4-2-3-1): Alisson (Jaros 79), Alexander-Arnold, Konate, Van Dijk (c), Tsimikas (Robertson 79), Gravenberch, Mac Allister (Szoboszlai 46), Jones (Endo 89), Salah (Diaz 73), Gakpo, Jota. Subs not used: Bradley, Quansah, Nunez, Gomez

Arne's post-match reaction: 'It definitely is [very satisfying, having the best winning start of any Liverpool boss with nine out of 10]. And it's actually also quite special if you know how many great managers Liverpool had. But I also said last week, I think, that I hope they don't only remember me in one, two, three, four, or five years only for this. We are hoping to do more special things than this. And it also says the luck I had that I inherited a very good squad and very good staff to continue getting the results that Jürgen [Klopp] had here as well.

He [Gravenberch] has certain characteristics to play in that position, and one of them is that he is really comfortable with the ball. Every time you play [it to] him, he knows what to do with it, so he is really good in his one or two-touch passes. But he is also very comfortable in turning away from his man so we can create an overload. But apart from that, where is the main focus for everyone? Probably if you make highlights of him, you're mainly going to show his offensive work. He is tall, he can run, strong in the duels. The positive for him in being in this position is if he played a bit higher up the pitch, everybody is always talking about his goals and assists that he needs to do more. Now in this position, that's not why we play him. But it's also very helpful for him to play in front of Virgil [van Dijk] and Ibou [Konate], to play next to Macca [Mac Allister] because it's a big help for him, those players as well.

Alisson is our clear No. 1; he is the best goalkeeper in the world. So, it's always a blow when he gets injured, for himself but also for us as a team. But the positive thing for the team is — and it's not only in the goalkeeper position but almost in every position — that we have a second option that is also really good. And Caoimh [Kelleher] has already shown that, so it is quite clear then that he is the No. 2. Otherwise, the last time Alisson was injured, I would have played Vit [Jaros], but I played Caoimh. So Caoimh is the No. 2 and did really well. It's very pleasing to see that even our third goalkeeper — because Caoimh was sick yesterday and today, of course — can have an impact on our results.'

Post-match notes

Arne Slot is the first Liverpool boss in history to win each of his first five away matches in charge. Vítězslav Jaros came off the bench to make his Reds debut following an injury to Alisson.

v Chelsea
Sunday, October 20th, 4.30pm

'YOU ARE ALWAYS LOOKING FOR PERFECTION EVEN THOUGH IT ISN'T REALLY ATTAINABLE'

Premier League

Good afternoon and welcome to Anfield for our Premier League fixture against Chelsea.

Going by the league table as things stand, Chelsea are the strongest opponents we have faced so far. Going into this weekend, they were in fourth place, having had a good start to the season and picking up some really good results along the way.

This should not come as any surprise, of course. Chelsea have a lot of good players, and they finished last season well also, so it makes sense that they will continue to develop and improve, and this is certainly happening right now. We have said repeatedly that there would be some big tests to come for us, and this is definitely one of them.

At the same time, it is also a big opportunity. Since we came together as a squad in pre-season, we have been developing ourselves, working incredibly hard to instil the methods that underpin the way that we want to play, and challenging ourselves to become better in all areas of the game.

That we have been able to keep on picking up results during this period is a real positive, as it can only enhance our own belief in what we are doing and give us confidence to take forward, something that can only help in periods like the one we are now entering when the games against strong opponents come thick and fast.

At the same time, we are aware that regardless of what the results or the current league table tell us, we also need to keep on improving. As a head coach, you are always looking for perfection even though you also know that perfection isn't really attainable, but the reality right now is that we still have a lot of work to do.

This is inevitable, of course. We are still only in our third month with the full squad together because so many of the players did not return until late July and early August due to their involvement in summer tournaments.

As I said, the fact that we have picked up as many points as we have since then is very promising, and it has given us a platform to build from in the coming weeks and months.

The one negative from our last game away to Crystal Palace is that we have lost Alisson Becker for the time being. No-one needs me to tell me how good a goalkeeper Alisson is or how well he has been performing this season, but I also do not think too many people will need reminding how good a goalkeeper Caoimhin Kelleher is or how well he has performed for us when called upon.

In an ideal world we would not get any injuries, but in any Premier League season it is inevitable that players will get injured, so it is vital that we have players like Caoimhin who have the quality and attitude to come into the team and make a positive impact. He has done this already this season, so hopefully he can do it again.

Finally, I would like to welcome Enzo Maresca, his

staff and players to Anfield. Enzo is doing a really good job at Chelsea, as he did at Leicester City previously, so he and his team will arrive here looking to make a mark. I actually saw during the week that Enzo had been complimentary about Anfield, and we will need the crowd here today to live up to the deserved reputation that it has.

Between us, if we can create a good atmosphere on the pitch by performing well, we can definitely make a difference.

Liverpool 2 Chelsea 1

Goals: Salah (29, pen), Jones (51)

Line-up (4-2-3-1): Kelleher, Alexander-Arnold (Gomez 81), Konate, Van Dijk (c), Robertson, Gravenberch, Jones (Mac Allister 81), Szoboszlai, Salah, Gakpo (Diaz 66), Jota (Nunez 30). Subs not used: Jaros, Endo, Quansah, Morton, Tsimikas

Arne's post-match reaction: 'Yeah, of course, I am [pleased] with the outcome. Because if you win, then you're always pleased about the outcome. In an ideal world we would've outplayed them completely. That's definitely not what we did. It was an equal game, in my opinion. There were phases in the game where we had to work really hard not to concede, but it's very pleasing to see that is also what we did.

I think we all saw the great block tackles Dominik [Szoboszlai] and Curtis [Jones] had – Curtis first half, Dominik second half.

Those moments are just as crucial as the goals we scored, and added to that, there were a lot of eventful decisions by the referee, which made it the game it was. I think if you're not a Liverpool supporter or Chelsea supporter, you really liked what you saw today. In the end, also if you are a Liverpool supporter, you liked what you saw today.

He [Jones] had a very good game. He had a difficult job to control Cole Palmer, who is an incredible player in my opinion. It's so difficult to defend him because he has so many qualities. Curtis did that really well today. In my opinion, he controlled him for most parts of the game; it's almost impossible to control a player like this for 90 minutes, but he was quite close to that. And then to even have an impact on the other side with a goal and two penalties that he was involved in; one of them was in the end disallowed by the VAR, but that shows you that he had a big impact on both sides of the pitch.

I think it was mostly the media that told us that this was our first big test. I think if you go to Old Trafford against a very strong team like [Manchester] United, that is definitely a test as well.'

Post-match notes

Ten wins in the first 11 games is the best start to a Liverpool season since Kenny Dalglish's men achieved the same record in 1990-91.

Wednesday, October 23rd, 8pm
UEFA Champions League,
RB Leipzig 0 Liverpool 1

Goal: Nunez (27)

Line-up (4-3-3): Kelleher, Alexander-Arnold (Gomez 75), Konate, Van Dijk (c), Tsimikas (Robertson 75), Szoboszlai, Gravenberch, Mac Allister, Salah (Diaz 63), Nunez (Jones 74), Gakpo. Subs not used: Jaros, Davies, Endo, Morton, Quansah, Nyoni

Arne's post-match reaction: 'I don't think we started the game really well in the first 10 or 15 minutes, but after that I liked a lot what I saw. Many, many, many times we played through their press, opened up their midfield, and went for an attack. That led to the first goal; that led to a few chances — more than a few — and then in the end it's a pity that you still need your two centre-backs to play such a big game and your goalkeeper to make two such important saves because a game like this should have been ours after 60, 70 minutes, and it wasn't. That's why the last 20 were still difficult for us.

I'm always happy when we score a goal, and I'm not that much into who scores it. It is always good to see all of our players scoring goals, and I think in the lead-up to the goal, Cody [Gakpo] and Mo [Salah] were just as important in the goal as Darwin [Nunez] was. What I liked from Darwin was that *he was also strong, comfortable on the ball, kept the ball a lot, fighting if he had to defend, so he made it a really difficult game for the two centre-backs of Leipzig. And then for him scoring, I think that is always nice for a striker to be on the scoresheet.*

If you play good teams, and if you play a pot one team in an away game, there will always be moments in the game that the other team has some moments as well, and I think one of them was from a corner kick. The way I looked at this game was that we had, for large parts of the game, total dominance, like in all the other games we played except for the one against Chelsea.

So, I am not worried at all about this game. I was a bit more worried, if you want to call it like this, after the Chelsea game. But this is how I like to see our team play: much more chances than the other team, much more ball possession, much more time freeing up the midfield from build-up. So, that was good, but I agree that if you were only there for the first 10 and the last 20 [minutes] that there were also difficult phases in the game. But that, at this level, is what happens in football.'

Post-match notes

Slot guided Liverpool to their sixth successive away win in all competitions, the club's best start to a season in that respect — and made it nine points out of nine in the revamped Champions League group phase.

Sunday, October 27th, 4.30pm
Premier League
Arsenal 2 Liverpool 2

Goals: Van Dijk (18), Salah (81)

Line-up (4-2-3-1): Kelleher, Alexander-Arnold, Konate, Van Dijk (c), Robertson (Tsimikas 63), Gravenberch, Mac Allister (Szoboszlai 63), Diaz (Gakpo 63), Jones (Endo 90+1), Salah, Nunez. Subs not used: Jaros, Davies, Gomez, Morton, Quansah

Arne's post-match reaction: 'Going two times behind against a very strong and good Arsenal team and then to get a point is pleasing to see, especially because we had to play an away game in Europe this week. We had one day less to recover and to prepare, and then to go two times behind with the fans being so loud and us coming back so strongly [in the] second half – because I think we deserved to be 2-1 down or one goal down at half-time – then is very pleasing to see that we had the energy and that we were so strong to fight ourselves back in the game [in the] second half, also because the ones that came in did really good but also that we were physically really strong today.

I think today was a big game for us again, just like last week against Chelsea, where he showed up with a goal and an assist also. That's also what you need if you are a big club – like we are and like Arsenal is – then you need these quality players *because if you don't have them, it's going to be quite difficult to get your results. It's something you need to have as a club to have these players that can make the difference for you, and Mo [Salah] was that today offensively. Although I think we have to give credit to Darwin [Nunez] and to Trent [Alexander-Arnold] as well in that goal.*

But for me the one that stood out today was? That's a question! I think [Ibrahima] Konate was also very good for us today. He doesn't always get the attention he deserves, in my opinion. He's asking to be the Man of the Match all the time, but he's coming closer and closer and closer to achieving that because I think he had a great performance today as well.

I know you guys like to talk about title contenders and where we are exactly in the league – that's also part of your job. The only thing I look at is, 'Can you get a result in a difficult away game as this one?' And the way we did it pleased me a lot, and we're only nine or 10 games into the season. But to see that we can compete with such a strong Arsenal team in their stadium, that is very pleasing to see. But what it exactly will lead towards in the end of the season, I cannot tell you yet.'

Post-match notes

For the first time under Slot's management the Reds conceded more than one goal but came from behind twice to sit second in the Premier League.

**Wednesday, October 30th, 7.30pm
Carabao Cup fourth round
Brighton & Hove Albion 2 Liverpool 3**

Goals: Gakpo (46, 63), Diaz (85)

Line-up (4-4-2): Jaros, Bradley, Gomez, Quansah (Konate 90+2), Robertson (c), Endo (Nyoni 64), Morton (Mac Allister 64), Gakpo (Salah 71), Diaz, Szoboszlai (Nunez 71), Jones. Subs not used: Kelleher, Van Dijk, Tsimikas, Young

Arne's post-match reaction: 'If you have to come here, you know it's going to be a difficult game because of the style of play, because of the recruitment they have here over the last few years. And then to get away from here with a result, with a win, is of course very pleasing. For the long term, I really liked what I see from players that haven't played that much this season yet, that they were able to play a similar style that we usually do and they brought quality into the game, so that makes it even harder for me to make line-ups in the upcoming weeks.

I think in the second half of last season he [Cody Gakpo] got a lot of goals already. He has been a good player for Liverpool for a long time now, and that's a good thing. For me, he is a regular starter. He is not starting every game, but he has started on a regular basis, and he is in a tough competition with Luis Diaz, who, in the moment he went on the left, also scored a goal. So, that's normal: if you play at a club like Liverpool, you *have got two quality players for many positions, and if you look at the way Joe Gomez played and also Jarell Quansah – who was maybe a bit unlucky with the goal we conceded because the overall performance I liked from them both as well – they are in competition with Virgil [van Dijk] and Ibou [Konate]. So that's what you have when you play at Liverpool, but for me, Cody has been a regular starter this season.*

It's only been 13 or 14 games or something like this, but it's been a very good start away from home but also at home, and we need good form on Saturday as well because we came here knowing they are a good team, and that's also what they showed today. So, we need to be on top of our game for Saturday again.

Everybody could see how important his [Jaros'] saves were. I think the first big chance of the game was for them, where he saved the one-versus-one, and in the second half, of course, we all remember one or two saves as well. But he also added to that how comfortable he was with the ball at his feet, making the right choices on when to go short and when to clip the ball towards the striker, and it helped for him the quality Jarell Quansah and Joe Gomez brought in build-up. So, I liked that triangle today a lot in ball possession.'

Post-match notes

The Reds earned a place in the quarter-finals of the Carabao Cup as Vitezslav Jaros made his full debut.

![L.F.C.]

NOV

2024

It was five wins out of five as the season picked up pace with Slot's men putting their foot on the gas in the Premier League and Champions League – no mean feat with some of the continent's most talented sides coming to town

Coming up:
2nd: Brighton & Hove Albion (PL) H
5th: Bayer Leverkusen (CL) H
9th: Aston Villa (PL) H
24th: Southampton (PL) A
27th: Real Madrid (CL) H

v Brighton & Hove Albion
Saturday, November 2nd, 3pm

'IF WE ARE TO WIN AGAIN, WE WILL HAVE TO PERFORM REALLY WELL AGAIN'

Premier League

Good afternoon and welcome to Anfield for our Premier League fixture against Brighton & Hove Albion.

Of course, it is only a few days since our teams last met, so there has not been too much time to digest the outcome, but the reality is that no matter how that game would have turned out, we would know that today's game would be another really tough one.

For the long term, on Wednesday night I really liked what I saw from the players who haven't played that much this season yet, that they were able to play a similar style that we usually do and they brought quality into the game. That makes it even harder for me to make line-ups in the upcoming weeks, but this is also something that I want.

The fact that we won will not make a difference today, though. What we earned in that tie was a place in the next round of the Carabao Cup, and that is very welcome, but it does not bring us any advantages in this fixture. If we are to win again, we will have to perform really well again.

We recognise the challenge that our opponents will bring, and this means there will be no shortcuts.

In recent seasons, Brighton have earned themselves a reputation for being an exciting, up-and-coming team, but I would say that they have now moved onto another level again, having established themselves as a top-level Premier League side. The fact that they go into this game in sixth place, having achieved some really good results already this season, only underlines this.

I would like to welcome Fabian Hürzeler, his players and staff, and everyone associated with the club to Anfield, having had the courtesy of a similar welcome at the AMEX Stadium in midweek.

I said in the build-up to that game that I really like Brighton's playing style, and this feeling has not changed in any way since then. If anything, it has become even stronger.

Like us, they are a club with a clear sense of identity and a lot of ambition. So we cannot say that we do not know what to expect today. We know them, and they know us. The difference this time, of course, is that the game takes place at Anfield in front of our fans, and this is a significant change which will hopefully help us as we continue making our way through a testing period with lots of fixtures in a short space of time.

I have been asked on a few occasions during this spell if I am learning new things about the players, but the truth is that I am learning new things all the time. This is normal after only a few months at a new club because it takes time to see everyone in various situations, but the big conclusion so far is that I could not be more pleased with the way the players are committing and adapting to a new way of working.

There is still much that we can and will improve. We are as aware as anyone that we are still a work in progress – as should be expected at this stage – but while this process is taking place, we have also been able to pick up some really positive results, both at home and in Europe, which are giving us a platform to build from.

The victory on Wednesday night was another good example of what I am talking about. Yes, there were elements of our game that we will need to be better at going forward, but there were also parts of our performance that were very pleasing, and this was why we were able to get the win.

Today I would like to see more of the same but with certain improvements. That is how we will continue to take the kind of steps forward that we are looking for. As always, though, we will look to take these steps together.

Liverpool 2 Brighton & Hove Albion 1

Goals: Gakpo (70), Salah (72)

Line-up (4-2-3-1): Kelleher, Alexander-Arnold, Konate (Gomez 46), Van Dijk (c), Tsimikas, Gravenberch, Mac Allister (Jones 66), Szoboszlai (Diaz 66), Gakpo, Salah (Bradley 90+1), Nunez (Endo 77). Subs not used: Jaros, Quansah, Robertson, Morton

Arne's post-match reaction: 'First of all, credit to Brighton, the way they showed up over here. They showed a lot of composure; they were not afraid to play. They play out from the back really well. A lot of energy without the ball. And we didn't show up at all in every part of the game, maybe except for the set-pieces part. But for the rest we were not there, and if you face a very good team like Brighton, it's not enough to run once, twice, or three times; you have to keep on running.

So, we changed a bit of tactics, but that had nothing to do with ball possession; that had nothing to do with us coming out stronger in the second half; the players showed a different attitude and different intensity. Therefore, I said a few things, and we showed a few things, but it wasn't that I was screaming or fuming around. It's just making sure the players understand that this was not enough, and I think they felt it themselves as well.

What I do like a lot is that last week, two times we came from one goal behind against Arsenal, 1-0 and 2-1, and two times we were able to fight ourselves back into the game. And in this game we were 1-0 down at half-time, which I think we deserved, and then to come back so strong against such a quality team, led by a few very good managers in the last few years, and then to come back the way we did gives me a lot of confidence.

But I also added after the game to the players that 45 minutes of the football we played in the first half will, in the end, punish you somewhere. So we need to show up from the start.'

Post-match notes

The win over Brighton saw Arne make history with eight wins from his first 10 Premier League games, something no other Liverpool boss has achieved.

November 2024

**v Bayer Leverkusen
Tuesday, November 5th, 8pm**

'THE MAXIMUM RESPECT WE CAN GIVE ANY FORMER PLAYER IS TO BE THE BEST LIVERPOOL WE CAN POSSIBLY BE'

Champions League group phase

Good evening and welcome to Anfield for our Champions League game against Bayer Leverkusen.

This is our last but one fixture before the international break as we come to the end of a really testing period, and our aim is simple – to carry on giving everything we can to keep on progressing on all fronts.

When this mini-period began in mid-October, a lot of people – including myself – said that it would be a spell in which we would find out a lot about where we are at as a team, and this has definitely turned out to be true.

Saturday's game against Brighton gave us some more information, and while most of it, particularly the result and second-half performance, was positive, we were also given a very clear warning of what we can look like if we allow our standards to drop.

Without wishing to puncture the joy that came with beating Brighton in the way that we did, we have no option but to recognise that the first half was not good enough and was actually a long way short of being good enough. I know what happened in the second half will give us positive memories, but we should not and cannot forget what happened in the opening 45 minutes.

The reason for this is that if you perform this way, it will punish you somewhere, especially when you have a run of fixtures in which the quality of opposition is so high.

Like Brighton, Bayer Leverkusen are a side which has the ability to hurt any opponent, so we have to be ready for this reality and face up to it with as much energy, quality, and intensity as we can produce.

Everyone in football was impressed with what Leverkusen did last season. How could you not be? To become champions of Germany is a wonderful achievement in itself, but to do so without losing a single game makes it even more remarkable.

They also had to show all of the characteristics of champions. There were games in which they were dominant, games in which they were not at their best but still found a way, and games in which their quality was so high that it was impossible not to view them as one of the strongest teams in Europe.

Of course, a lot of this is down to their head coach, Xabi Alonso, someone who I know does not need any introduction to our supporters, who recall him with incredible fondness for what he did as a player at Liverpool. I was not a Liverpool supporter, but I have always been a football fan, and anyone from my generation who falls into this category would share this admiration.

Xabi was a top-class player, and he is proving himself to be of the same level as a manager. I would like to welcome him back to Anfield, and I know that in doing so I will be in tune with the feelings of everyone who is inside the stadium tonight. In doing this, though, we are all aware that there will be no sentimentality from him, and this means that there cannot be any from us.

The maximum respect we can give any former player is to be the best Liverpool that we can possibly be with no quarter asked and no quarter given.

As I have already said, this was definitely our approach during the second half on Saturday, and it brought us a really important win. It was not just the case on the pitch either. It was exactly the same in the stands, and the incredible noise which was produced was definitely the loudest that I have experienced since I have been at Liverpool.

Perhaps it would be greedy to look for a repeat, but in the spirit of there being no harm in asking, it would be wonderful if collectively we could look to reach those kinds of levels again. Energy in the stands brings energy among the players and vice versa. It is a virtuous circle that I know has served this club incredibly well over the years, so the more that we can bring it to the stadium, the better.

Liverpool 4 Bayer Leverkusen 0

Goals: Diaz (61, 83, 90+2), Gakpo (63)

Line-up (4-3-3): Kelleher, Alexander-Arnold (Bradley 81), Konate (Quansah 88), Van Dijk (c), Tsimikas (Robertson 80), Jones (Szoboszlai 73), Gravenberch, Mac Allister, Salah, Gakpo (Nunez 80), Diaz. Subs not used: Jaros, Davies, Endo, Morton, Gomez

Arne's post-match reaction: 'Like many times now, managers change their game plan when they come to Anfield or when they play us — that's also what we saw today. We've seen a lot of games from Leverkusen, but I've never seen [Victor] Boniface playing from the left. So, they played without a nine, and that's why they overloaded the midfield a lot.

It was quite difficult to press them high. But the good thing was that we hardly conceded anything, and I think during the first half if there were chances, they were for us. But [in the] second half we could adjust to the game plan of the first half; we took a bit more risks, we were better with the ball as well. Normally they defend more in a 5-2-3; now they defended in a 4-4-2, so they changed quite a lot, and we could adjust to that at half-time.

Not only the people in Colombia like and love Lucho [Diaz], the fans of Liverpool love him a lot as well. I heard many times the fans singing his song. And the manager likes him a lot as well — I don't love him, but I like him a lot! In the Premier League and the Champions League, you have to play so many games at the highest level, and it's not always possible for every player to play every game, especially in certain positions. So, if you are a centre-back, normally you run not as much as a left-winger or a full-back or a midfielder — and especially our wingers. But because you all look at the goals Lucho scored and the goals Cody [Gakpo] scored, I also look at the fact how hard they track back, how much they have to defend. I ask a lot from them, so that's why sometimes we have to rotate them. But Lucho, for me, is a starter. And I said this three days ago about Cody as well — he's, for me, a starter also.

Arne Slot

We have to work really hard, play with an incredible high intensity to win our games, and that has a lot to do with teams – I heard Bayer Leverkusen saying this as well – they think, and I have to agree with them, that Anfield is the best place to play in, one of the nicest stadiums to play in, and against a very good team. So, every team that plays against us is in the top of their game. And if you want to win that, you always have to be consistent in your intensity, and that's not always easy, but that is what's needed. And if we can keep producing that, then it's still not easy, but then we get our wins in, and that is what we want.

If you work at any club around the world, there is always pressure. So for some clubs or some managers, there is pressure not to go down. For some, they have to win a lot. In our position, there is always pressure. This is the pressure we give ourselves as well because if you work for Liverpool or play at Liverpool, as a player or a manager, you know the manager is probably going to come next, and so many other great players have set the standard so high over here, so it always feels there is a bit of pressure. But we also embrace this because that is also what we want. We want to be there, where we are now; we want to compete for everything, and, therefore, you have to accept that if you work here or play here that there is pressure.'

Post-match notes

Luis Diaz scored his first Liverpool hat-trick as the Reds claimed a comfortable win to stay top of the 36-team Champions League group with four wins from four.

v Aston Villa
Saturday, November 9th, 8pm

'THE RESULTS WE HAVE ACHIEVED HAVE BEEN REALLY POSITIVE BUT NOW IS NOT A TIME TO REFLECT'

Premier League

Good evening, and welcome to our Premier League home game against Aston Villa, a fixture which will bring an end to a really tough spell before the international break.

There is no doubt that the results we have achieved in this period have been really positive, but now is not the time to reflect on those. Our focus has to be on continuing this form, not just tonight but going forward also, because the challenges will continue to come our way, and this means we have to be ready for them.

Aston Villa are the latest one, and they have shown already this season that they have the quality to be a contender at the top end of the table, just as they were last season when they qualified for the Champions League for the first time. This was clearly a big achievement for them, but the most important thing was that it was also very much deserved.

I would like to welcome Unai Emery, his staff, and the players and supporters of Aston Villa to Anfield. They will come here, of course, with the objective of getting a good result for their club, so again, this is something that we have to be prepared for, and as part of this, we should not read anything into their last couple of results.

I do not say this because I think results do not matter; the opposite is actually true. But we also know from experience how hard it is to get good results at this level, and when this is the case, it means that it would not take too much for them to go the other way. The margins can be this narrow.

We only have to go back one week to the visit of Brighton to Anfield, when we had to play with an incredible high intensity to turn that game around against a very strong opponent.

This is what it takes when a league is so competitive because the margins for error do not allow for shortcuts. We could have lost, we could have drawn, but we found a way to win, and this pleases me a lot, especially as we deserved the three points in the end.

That we then followed this up with a victory against Bayer Leverkusen is even more pleasing because I said at the start of this spell that the biggest test would be playing games in the Premier League and the Champions League in the space of a few days.

This is not an easy thing to do, and it is also something that the team had not done last season because they were in the Europa League, but they have shown that they are ready for the challenge.

We would be the first to acknowledge the help that we have received from our supporters, though. Of course I knew about the atmosphere at Anfield before I came to Liverpool, but to experience it at its best as head coach is an incredible experience, particularly when I am able to see the positive effect that it has on our players.

In the last two home games the atmosphere has been special. In moments when we have really needed them, the fans have given us the extra push that we required, and in general the support has been unbelievable. I would never like to ask too much of people who have already given so much, but if the atmosphere even comes close today, it will help us a lot.

Finally, with this being Remembrance weekend, we will use today's fixture to pay our respects to those who have died in conflict. The sacrifices that have been made in these situations should never be forgotten and nor should loved ones who have been left behind.

I know there will be people at Anfield today who will have very personal reasons for reflecting and remembering, so the thoughts of all of us are with you.

Liverpool 2 Aston Villa 0

Goals: Nunez (20), Salah (84)

Line-up (4-2-3-1): Kelleher, Alexander-Arnold (Bradley 25), Konate, Van Dijk (c), Robertson, Gravenberch, Mac Allister (Endo 87), Jones (Szoboszlai 65), Diaz, Salah, Nunez (Gakpo 65). Subs not used: Jaros, Gomez, Tsimikas, Quansah, Morton

Arne's post-match reaction: 'If you win, it mostly doesn't get better than that, and yeah, you know, if you win the amount of games we do, you can be ahead. It's not sure yet in this league because Arsenal, City, Chelsea, all these clubs that are playing in this league, they are able to win so many games as well, and that's what they have shown in the last few seasons. So, we are only focused on ourselves, and then a win against a very good team like Villa, who have done so well in the last few years, is always important.

If you play at Anfield in front of your own fans, you should always be motivated, and that's what they've been for the time I have been here now and probably the years before as well. So, you should not need motivation from a result on another pitch, and that's also not what I felt today with the players. Maybe the fans feel different; I don't know. You'd have to ask them.

It was definitely a big week, but every game is a big week. We play so many games in all these competitions against strong opponents, so hopefully we will have a lot of these weeks to come because these weeks are mostly big if you are competing for something, and that is what we are doing at the moment. We are competing, trying to compete for the league, trying to compete for the Champions League, and trying to compete for the cups we are in as well. We also know it's a long season where we have to continuously be on top of our game because the likes of Arsenal, City, and Chelsea and all these other clubs are able to win just as many games as we did in the first 15 to 16 games.'

Post-match notes

The Reds made it nine wins from 11 to go five points clear at the top of the Premier League.

Sunday, November 24th, 2pm
Premier League
Southampton 2 Liverpool 3

Goals: Szoboszlai (30), Salah (65, 83 pen)

Line-up (4-2-3-1): Kelleher, Bradley, Konate, Van Dijk (c), Robertson,
Gravenberch, Jones (Mac Allister 62), Szoboszlai, Gakpo (Diaz 62),
Salah, Nunez (Endo 90). Subs not used: Jaros, Gomez, Quansah,
Morton, Elliott, Davies

Arne's post-match reaction: "*Over the moon' is a bit exaggerating*
but of course we are really happy. Especially because after an
hour we were 2-1 down. Maybe that wasn't a reflection of
how the first hour went because I think we dominated the whole
game, which is not that easy. Maybe you think we played the
number 20 [team in the league standings], and this is what we
expect, but I've seen many games of Southampton that they were
dominating the game. In the end, if you're 2-1 down after an
hour, you are maybe over the moon if you win 3-2.

We always know we can trust him [Salah] if things are difficult
for us. After we went 2-1 down, I didn't really feel that was
the moment we should score in. Then out of a fantastic pass
from Ryan Gravenberch, though [we did]. But the timing of the
run and the way Mo finished it was special, and that helped
us really [get] back into the game, of course. It's normal if you

score at 2-2; it helps you back in the game, but we needed that goal maybe to play the last 25 minutes that we played because then for me it was a matter of time before we scored a goal. In the first hour we dominated possession without really creating that much. In the last half-hour we were dominating – or the last 25 minutes – with creating some chances.

I think what I do as a manager is I want to know their style of play. Sometimes it makes a bit of a difference if a No.9 is high and tall or fast or slow. So, it makes a bit of a difference, but I don't think they changed their playing style. Not in the way they lined up as a 5-4-1 and also not in the way they like to play, because the first goal we scored was from them trying to bring the ball out from the back, which didn't happen a lot for them today. And that did happen a lot in other games because I showed the players yesterday how many times Southampton can play through a press. But today I think that part of our game was quite good; we were really aggressive without the ball.

That is the difference... this league asks a lot from every player every weekend, and then if you then play in Europe, that's not always easy. Only a few teams in England have shown they can do this. Liverpool have shown it in the past for many seasons.'

Post-match notes

Slot equalled the record for the fewest games for a manager to win 10 Premier League matches (12).

v Real Madrid
Wednesday, November 27th, 8pm

'WE KNOW WHEN WE APPLY OURSELVES THE RIGHT WAY WE CAN BE COMPETITIVE AGAINST ANYONE'

Champions League group phase

Good evening and welcome to Anfield for our UEFA Champions League fixture against Real Madrid, a game which I know will have created excitement when the draw was first made back in August given the history of both clubs in European competition. It goes without saying that Real are a great club.

Their recent record in both La Liga and the Champions League shows that this is a special period for them, even by their own incredibly high standards.

Our starting point is to respect this because nothing else would make sense. It would certainly be strange if we went into this game thinking they are anything but a top side.

At the same time, we have earned the right to have confidence in ourselves. The work that the players have done up to now has put us in the position that we are in – both at home and in Europe – so we know that when we apply ourselves the right way, stick to our principles, and believe in what we are trying to do, we can be competitive against anyone.

We are enjoying the situation that we are in at the moment and recognise the potential that exists, but we also know that it is still very early in the season. As things stand, we have played less than one-third of our Premier League fixtures, and tonight's game will take us just past the halfway point in the Champions League group.

Yes, a lot of football has been played, and we are happy with the points we have taken in both competitions, but there is a lot, lot more still to come. Now isn't the time to look back; it is the time to look forward with an ongoing sense of what we still have to do.

This is something that Real have shown themselves to be world leaders at. Yes, they are always aware of what they have done but mainly from the perspective of what they have to do next. If this approach is good enough for them, it is definitely good enough for everyone else.

I know it sounds boring, but I will not apologise for repeating that we will be taking every game as it comes. The alternative really wouldn't be logical, especially given how quickly matches come around when you are playing Champions League and Premier League.

The next game is literally the most important one. It is a chance to maintain standards, to increase belief, and to take more points, which means there is no need to look any further ahead when there is a challenge right in front of you.

I would like to welcome Carlo Ancelotti, his staff, and the players and supporters of Real to Anfield. Carlo knows English football, and he also understands what football means in this part of the country, having managed Everton, so he will bring a wealth of knowledge and experience with him.

He also comes with an incredibly strong squad that has a phenomenal record of success and which shows no signs of easing up.

The easy – and stupid – mistake to make would be to look at the current standards in the Champions League and believe Real's threat has diminished. The reality is the leaves have only just fallen from the trees.

How many times have clubs like Real found themselves in this kind of position in autumn only for it to feel like a trick of the mind by the time we reach spring? It is a story almost as old as football itself. For us, it is about recognising and embracing the excitement of a week in which we will host both the champions of Spain and the champions of England at Anfield. Again, these represent opportunities for us to continue with our work and a chance also for our crowd to do what it does best.

With every passing home game, I have been able to enjoy the Anfield atmosphere more and more, and I know that these are occasions when the supporters need no second invitation to get behind the team, so I am really looking forward to that.

Liverpool 2 Real Madrid 0

Goals: Mac Allister (52), Gakpo (76)

Line-up (4-3-3): Kelleher, Bradley (Gomez 87), Konate, Van Dijk, Robertson, Jones (Szoboszlai 83), Gravenberch, Mac Allister, Salah, Nunez (Gakpo 68), Diaz. Subs not used: Jaros, Davies, Alexander-Arnold, Elliott, Endo, Morton, Quansah

Arne's post-match reaction: 'I liked a lot what I saw. Of course not everything. I think we controlled the first half with creating a few chances, but I also thought we were still a bit sloppy, so we lost the ball in very easy situations, or we forced it a bit too much. I said, 'Try to be even more patient; let the gaps open up instead of forcing them.' Then it helps if, [in] the first seven minutes after half-time, I think we had total dominance; they even didn't come across the halfway line. If you score a goal like this, then we were flying, if you want to put it like this.

I think it's always good to win a game, and especially a big game like this, because you know you face so many quality players. For me, it would even mean more if we go into the later stages of the tournament because this is such a strange and different set-up in the Champions League that it's difficult to judge how important these wins are. If we arrive in the last 16 or the quarter-finals or wherever we can arrive and we face them again and then we are able to beat them, that would be maybe a bigger statement than this. But we are definitely happy with the win; let that be clear.

I think it's nice for him [Bradley], nice for his family, nice for us, but it's also very nice for the Academy that a player that comes through the ranks at the Academy does so well. And not only him – Caoimh [Kelleher] was outstanding today, Curtis [Jones] was outstanding today. Probably all of them were outstanding, but to have three Academy players in your team doing so well is also a big compliment for the Academy this club has. And Conor did very well. But I'm totally not surprised by him doing so well because he showed this already last season and showed this in this season in training sessions and in games as well. So, very nice for him.

I think every decision I have to make is a difficult one, because we have so many quality players. I've been clear about that situation, but tonight shouldn't be about that; it should be about Caoimh being so important for us. It was a big moment for him also, I think; if you see Mbappe behind the ball, I thought probably what everybody thought – and what everybody also thought when Mo [Salah] stepped up – 'This ball is probably going to go in.' And he saved it, so it was a big moment for him, a special moment for him. So, let that be the headlines and not the other thing I was quite clear about one or two weeks ago.

I don't think we transformed that much; we adjusted a bit. Here they are used to playing a final or to be up there with all the great teams in Europe. This team has always been there. We are only five games in, in a new format, so we are happy where we are, but we are not getting carried away by only winning in a group-stage game.'

Post-match notes

Liverpool maintained their flawless Champions League record with five wins out of five and just one goal conceded, and they finally beat Real Madrid after failing to beat the holders in the last eight meetings in the tournament. Caoimhin Kelleher's second-half penalty save from Kylian Mbappe was crucial.

DEC

2024

The hectic December schedule saw the Reds go unbeaten with a statement victory over last season's champions a highlight – and 17 goals in five away games showed Arne Slot's men to be a force to be reckoned with wherever they played

Coming up:
1st: Manchester City (PL) H
4th: Newcastle United (PL) A
10th: Girona (CL) A
14th: Fulham (PL) H
18th: Southampton (CC) A
22nd: Tottenham Hotspur (PL) A
26th: Leicester City (PL) H
29th: West Ham United (PL) A

v Manchester City
Sunday, December 1st, 4pm

'WITHIN THIS RIVALRY WE CAN DEFINITELY FIND ROOM TO RESPECT THEIR ACHIEVEMENTS'

Premier League

Good afternoon and welcome to Anfield for our Premier League fixture against Manchester City, the second time in a matter of days that we will meet the reigning champions of a major European league.

Let me start by saying Wednesday was a special night for this club. To defeat a team like Real Madrid, so many things have to come together — the performance of the players, the atmosphere created by the crowd, the preparation, the desire. It was all there. This is not to say it was perfect because as a coach you are always striving for a perfection that might not even exist, but all of the ingredients you would want were in place.

I liked a lot of what I saw. Again, not everything, but a lot. One of the things I liked most was that everyone from players to supporters saw the victory for what it was, and that is another step forward on the road to where we want to be. This isn't to play the win down or to make it less important.

But as I said afterwards, it was a group stage win and not a victory in the later stages or the final. Of course we can enjoy it, and we did enjoy it, but we know also that there is still work to be done.

It is also worth remembering that Real remain the best team in Europe. They won the Champions League last June, and this makes them holders. It is a similar situation with today's opponents, Manchester City, who are the holders of the Premier League, having won the title four years in a row.

The calibre of these teams speak for itself, and that is why this is such an exciting week, with us being able to play both of them in a matter of days.

I would like to welcome Pep Guardiola, his staff, and the players and supporters of Manchester City to Anfield. In terms of trophies won, there is no question that City have been a dominant force in English football for several seasons.

Yes, they are our rivals, but even within this rivalry we can definitely find room to respect their achievements and qualities.

It is an interesting time to play City because so many are questioning them at the moment. I am not one of them. This is not to ignore their recent results because clearly they have not been of the usual standard, but City still have one of the best managers in the world – if not the best manager in the world – numerous top-class players, and a culture of success, which means they cannot be written off even in times of adversity.

To be very clear, they remain one of the best sides not only in this country but also in the world, and we have prepared for this fixture on that basis. Of course we get to take our own belief into the game, and we will definitely do that, but we also arrive with the knowledge that our performance will have to be as good as, if not even better than, it was on Wednesday night.

We should not be surprised that we are in a good position, though. The squad that I inherited is one that has been high-performing for several seasons. It is not new to them to be challenging the likes of City and Real Madrid. It is what they have done for some time. But the challenge for them − for us − is not only to keep challenging; it is to show that we can continue improving in everything that we do. This is what the very best teams do. They do not stop and admire their work. They keep on pushing themselves.

Finally and importantly, today is a day when Liverpool FC as a club will show our support for the LGBTQ+ community by demonstrating our backing of Stonewall's Rainbow Laces campaign. This is something that we do proudly and passionately because football is for everyone and has to be for everyone.

Liverpool 2 Manchester City 0

Goals: Gakpo (12), Salah (78, pen)

Line-up (4-2-3-1): Kelleher, Alexander-Arnold (Quansah, 72) Gomez, Van Dijk (c), Robertson, Gravenberch, Mac Allister, Salah (Jones, 84), Szoboszlai, Gakpo (Nunez, 72), Diaz (Elliott, 90). Subs not used: Jaros, Davies, Endo, Morton, Nyoni.

Arne's post-match reaction: 'Playing against Real Madrid, playing against Man City, teams that have been and are so good, with managers that have won so many trophies, it's always nice to come out in both situations as a winner. But the reason why these teams won so many things is that they weren't able to win once or twice; they were able to win every three days. So, we're really happy with these two wins, but we also understand if we want to achieve more than this, then winning once or twice — even against these big teams — is not enough to win anything in the end of the season.

If you want to win anything, it's all about consistency. These teams — like Madrid, like City, but I saw Arsenal yesterday and I saw Chelsea today — they are all capable of getting the same winning streak as we have, so let's not get carried away.

It's all about consistency until the end of the season, keeping the players fit, keeping them playing with this much energy. And like you probably saw today, I only had five defenders available. So to win something in the end, there's such a long way to go and so many challenges to take. But it's good that we are capable of winning against these teams in our own style.

I've watched this game so many times... I always made sure I could watch this game, and it's always been great games. So, maybe for the fans that were neutral they liked it that it stayed 1-0 and it was tight until the end.'

Post-match notes

The victory saw Liverpool go nine points clear at the top of the Premier League and left defending champions Manchester City 11 points adrift of the summit.

Wednesday, December 4th, 7.30pm
Premier League
Newcastle United 3 Liverpool 3

Goals: Jones (50), Salah (68, 83)

Line-up (4-2-3-1): Kelleher, Quansah, Gomez (Alexander-Arnold 67), Van Dijk (c), Robertson, Gravenberch (Szoboszlai 67), Mac Allister, Gakpo (Diaz 67), Jones, Salah, Nunez. Subs not used: Jaros, Endo, Morton, Elliott, Nallo, Nyoni

Arne's post-match reaction: 'There were moments in the game where you thought if we could come away from here with a draw, it would be a good result, but those moments were mainly in the first half. In the second half, especially after we scored for 1-1, I thought we were really impressive. We created so many opportunities, good chances. Then, one minute before the end, being 3-2 up, it feels like a disappointment to drop two points.

I think Mo [Salah] had a massive impact on the game. Dom [Szoboszlai] came in really well, Lucho [Diaz] also, but I think in general in the second half we played much, much better than the first half. In the first half we had a lot of problems with their intensity, aggressive playing style without the ball – aggressive in a good way. We tried to cope with it, but every time we touched them we got a yellow, and that doesn't really help for us to be intense then as well. But we give credit to them; they were more intense than us. They forced us into too many mistakes. It wasn't that difficult for us to be better in the second half with the ball, and that's what we were. Maybe it was difficult for them to keep the intensity of the first 45 minutes going, and as a result of that, or of all of these things, we dominated the second half.

He [Salah] plays in a very good team that provides him with good opportunities, and then he is able to do special things. What makes him even more special for me is before we scored for 1-1, you thought, 'He is not playing his best game today,' but then to come up with an assist, two goals, having a shot against the bar, and being a constant threat within a half-hour — that is something not many players can do if they've played the first hour like he did. So, that is also what makes him special, apart from if you just look at the goals. His finishing is so clinical. A special player, but that's what we all know.

To go away to Newcastle is such a difficult game to play, and they have so much quality throughout the whole squad, but especially up front as well. So that they are able to score a goal, that's not a surprise for me, and especially the first one — what a finish that was. Ours was a great finish as well, but that shot from Isak, I don't even know if Caoimh [Kelleher] saw that.'

Post-match notes

Mo Salah made it 37 different games where he's both scored and assisted in the same Premier League match, going top of the list ahead of Wayne Rooney.

Tuesday, December 10th, 5.45pm
UEFA Champions League
Girona 0 Liverpool 1

Goal: Salah (63, pen)

Line-up (4-3-3): Alisson, Alexander-Arnold, Gomez, Van Dijk (c), Robertson, Jones (Elliott 76), Szoboszlai, Gravenberch, Salah, Nunez (Gakpo 71), Diaz (Endo 89). Subs not used: Jaros, Kelleher, Quansah, McConnell, Norris

Arne's post-match reaction: 'If you ask me about all the six games, I'm really pleased with all the results. I am really pleased with the five [other] games with the way we played. I'm far from pleased about the performance tonight.

If you play against a team that has such a good idea about football, knows how to bring the ball out from the back – like some other teams we faced recently, like [Manchester] City or Real Madrid – then you need to be so intense if you want to make it difficult for them. But if every time you are waiting a few seconds before you press, and if you do press, you are so easily outplayed, then this team can cause you a lot of problems. That's what they've shown throughout the whole Champions League campaign, except for [against] PSV Eindhoven away.

I almost feel sorry for them because they deserved so much more in this Champions League campaign than the three points they *have until now. But we have an incredible goalkeeper. The other part was every time we lost the ball we were not aggressive enough, so every time we lost the ball they could almost every time go all the way to our goal, having a shot or a blocked shot, and then we could attack again. Hardly any control at all over the game; maybe the second half was a bit better, but then I am trying to be positive.*

I think every striker all around the world has periods where every ball goes in, and sometimes he has a period where you try so hard but you're not able to score. The good thing is that we have many players that can score for us – today Mo [Salah] again. I would have loved to see Darwin score because I think every striker wants to score [and] needs goals – that's why I kept him in for quite a long time. He was a threat, but unfortunately he couldn't score. Yes, Alisson made a lot of saves, but I think if you make highlights of this game, we will all see a few chances that we had as well, which is normal. What is not normal is that we concede so many chances.'

Post-match notes

Liverpool virtually assured themselves of a spot in the knockout phase of the Champions League with their sixth win from six. Mo Salah scored his 46th Champions League goal while Alisson returned after a spell of injury.

v Fulham
Saturday, December 14th, 3pm

'WE NEED TO MAINTAIN THIS TOGETHERNESS AS THERE ARE BIG CHALLENGES AHEAD'

Premier League

Good afternoon and welcome to Anfield for our Premier League fixture against Fulham.

A lot has happened since we last played at home – we have drawn a tough game away to Newcastle, had the Merseyside derby postponed due to bad weather, and then travelled to Girona, where we continued our good results in the Champions League without producing the kind of performance that we know we are capable of.

In this respect, Girona was a funny situation. The league table made for really positive reading, and the result was another good one, particularly as we also kept our fifth clean sheet in that competition, but at the same time we all knew that we could and should have played better.

This isn't being overly critical. It is about us knowing the standards that we have to maintain and not allowing them to drop. The reason for this is simple – we are playing in competitions at home and abroad that have so many quality teams, and it does not take much of a drop-off to make life difficult. For this reason, it makes sense to always be self-critical and to recognise when improvement is needed because by doing this you can resolve issues before they become a problem.

Having said this, the bigger picture is that we have put ourselves in a good position in both the Champions League and the Premier League, and as we arrive in mid-December, we know that the opportunity exists to keep on pushing on.

This is credit to the players, the staff, and the supporters because it has been a collective effort to get here, and we will need to maintain this togetherness going forward as there are some big challenges ahead.

The first one arrives today with a Fulham team which is performing really well again this season. Sometimes teams can go under the radar because the focus is on other clubs for whatever reason, and it feels like this has happened with Fulham, who have gone about their business quietly and effectively, picking up some very impressive results and establishing themselves in the top half of the table.

They showed what they are capable of once again last weekend with a hard-earned draw against a very strong Arsenal team, so we definitely know what to expect. I would like to welcome Marco Silva, his players and staff, and the Fulham supporters to Anfield for what we expect to be a really competitive game.

It goes without saying that the spell we are in is a testing one for all clubs because of the number of games we have in a short space of time, so it is positive that players are starting to return to the squad after periods on the sidelines. Federico Chiesa and Diogo Jota have both stepped up training in recent days, Alisson Becker came back into the team in midweek, and Harvey Elliott came on during the second half, with James McConnell also being on the bench. Others are continuing with their recovery work at AXA, and we look forward to having them back because we will need them.

Alisson performed like he had never been away in Girona, and this is credit to him for the hard work he has put in and also to the staff who have worked with him. At the same time, though, we should not and will not overlook the contribution that was made by Caoimhin Kelleher during the period when Alisson was not available to us.

The standards he set for himself and the performances he produced for us underline both his quality as a goalkeeper and his high levels of professionalism. It is not an exaggeration in any way to say Caoimhin is one of the reasons why we are in the position that we are in.

We have two really good goalkeepers who both play to a really high level, and as I said at the start of these notes, it is so, so important that we continue to hold ourselves to the highest standards in all positions, on and off the pitch, because this is the only way to keep making progress.

Liverpool 2 Fulham 2

Goals: Gakpo (47), Jota (86)

Line-up (4-3-3): Alisson, Alexander-Arnold (Jota 79), Gomez, Van Dijk (c), Robertson, Gravenberch, Jones (Quansah 70), Szoboszlai (Elliott 79), Gakpo (Nunez 70), Diaz, Salah. Subs not used: Kelleher, Endo, Nyoni, Chiesa, Morton

Arne's post-match reaction: 'I think it is exactly the opposite from the Girona game, where I was pleased with the result but not with the performance. I was only pleased with the result. Now I am very, very, very happy about the performance [today]. I couldn't have asked for more, but of course not with the result because if you drop points in a home game with Fulham, that is definitely not what you expect or what you want. Being two times a goal down, so many things go against you except for one thing, and that is our players and our fans, who were outstanding today.

I think what the team showed today, the character, that's also what Robbo [Robertson] showed. Sometimes if you get a kick like this, two studs on a knee, that can hurt for a few minutes. Then, if you just keep on running, it gets better and better, and that's what we were hoping for. Not least because I only had one defender on the bench, who was not a left full-back as well. So, we were hoping he was managing to come through it, and I think he did quite well, but the moment I noticed he wasn't completely himself was the one time they put the ball in behind and he started running. He was just able to head it back to Ali [Alisson Becker], but I thought, 'Okay, let's see how this continues,' and I think it was quite quickly afterwards where he conceded the red card. Nothing to blame on him; [it was] character that he wanted to continue because he got quite a hard knock on his knee. Unfortunately, it led to a red card that was a deserved red card.

I was impressed, like everyone who was in the stadium or saw the game. Ryan [Gravenberch] did outstanding again today.

Without the ball, he was mostly in our last line, had to play sometimes against a nine, against wingers who are really fast. And with the ball, he came into the midfield. An outstanding performance from him. But if we only highlight him, I don't think I give enough credit to all the other ones that played around him. I couldn't have asked for more. Dominated the game, more ball possession with 10 men, more chances created – everything you want. Unfortunately for us, maybe the only chance they got with [us having] 10 men led to a goal – that sometimes happens.

If you are one goal up, you might consider to defend with a lot of players, so then I might have considered to bring immediately a defender in. But if you are one goal down, you see differently. So first you take a look at the tactics board and you think, 'This might be a good option.' That's what we did for five minutes. But then looking at it, it looked better on a tactics board than on the pitch with Cody [Gakpo] being a left-back! So, we changed that after five minutes, and our message cut across, I think, even better at half-time. And then it helps if you immediately score the 1-1. What doesn't help – we had great momentum – [was] that the game was again delayed for three, four, or five minutes immediately after we scored the goal because they were on the ground, and that happened a bit too much for us to keep the momentum going.'

Post-match notes

Andy Robertson received a red card in the 17th minute, Liverpool's first of the season.

🏆

Wednesday, December 18th, 8pm
Carabao Cup quarter-final
Southampton 1 Liverpool 2

Goals: Nunez (23), Elliott (32)

Line-up (4-3-3): Kelleher, Alexander-Arnold (c) (Chiesa 46), Endo, Quansah, Gomez, Nyoni (Danns 86), Morton, Mac Allister (McConnell 63), Gakpo (Jota 63), Nunez, Elliott. Subs not used: Jaros, Tsimikas, Nallo, Ngumoha

Arne's post-match reaction: 'Harvey [Elliott] already had a good impact in the game at the weekend against Fulham, so it was good to see he is able to play 90 today and even score a goal. Started him off on the right; I felt he almost got a bit bored and didn't touch the ball a lot, so after 15-20 minutes we changed his [position] and were playing him in the midfield. We know he is a better midfielder than he is a winger, but we had to do it like this. So that was pleasing to see.

If I have to give someone a big compliment, it should be Wata Endo because in a different position, playing such a good game in these circumstances, that shows you what a quality player he is, but mainly maybe what kind of mentality and personality he has. Good to see them both, but I think it was not only them.

I think this club is known for this talent from the Academy. I heard the fans singing for Trent [Alexander-Arnold], the song about the Scouser. I don't know exactly what they sing, but it *probably has to do with him coming from the Academy as well. We have already a few starters from our academy, and to see these players that train with us on a daily basis, we know their quality, so it's nice to see that they show [it] on a Premier League level that they can easily play at this level.*

The thing for them is, it's not about easily playing at this level, but you have to compete with Mo [Salah], Virgil [van Dijk], and all these kind of players. It's not enough to be good enough to play at this level; you have to be good enough to play for Liverpool, and that is probably the next step they have to make. But they've showed today that these players are capable of playing at a Premier League level, that's for sure.

I don't know if we saw it the same, but I think what I saw is what you can expect. If a player [Chiesa] is out for five or six months, you cannot expect [too much]. I saw ups and downs. I saw some really good moments and I saw some moments where I felt like, 'Okay, you can do better than this.' For me, that's completely normal if a player has been out for so long and plays his first game in five or six months.'

Post-match notes

Arne Slot watched the game from the stands as he served a one-game touchline ban but was able to hand Harvey Elliott his first start of the season.

Sunday, December 22, 4.30pm
Premier League
Tottenham Hotspur 3 Liverpool 6

Goals: Diaz (23, 85), Mac Allister (36), Szoboszlai (45+1), Salah (54, 61)

Line-up (4-2-3-1): Alisson, Alexander-Arnold, Gomez, Van Dijk (c), Robertson, Gravenberch, Mac Allister (Jones 68), Szoboszlai, Gakpo (Jota 68), Salah (Elliott 87), Diaz (Nunez 87). Subs not used: Kelleher, Endo, Nyoni, Quansah, Tsimikas

Arne's post-match reaction: 'Until 60, 65 minutes, I really, really, really enjoyed what I saw. Of course, we were caught one time bringing the ball out from the back, and that immediately led to a goal for Tottenham. You think if we would have gone into the dressing room with a 2-1, that would not have done justice to all the chances we had — that's why I was quite happy with the fact that we scored the 3-1. Then 4-1, 5-1, incredible display. But then you also saw that no matter how much quality players have, if they think they don't have to run anymore in this league, especially against Tottenham because they are so good with the ball as well, they immediately start to create, and that's what they did, and they scored two goals. I was happy that the sixth one went in, to be fair.

It was very good — maybe it was our best performance away

from home, although I really liked what I saw against Man United as well. It was total dominance, and we outplayed them many, many times also, so that was a very good away game as well. Today, apart from scoring six goals, I think we could have even scored more. It's always like this; you don't score every chance, although Tottenham almost did because the first three chances were a goal. Mo [Salah] and Lucho [Diaz], they were both with two goals, maybe the ones that stand out in terms of scoring two. But I think we would not do justice to Dom's [Szoboszlai] performance if we don't name him as well because, apart from his attacking things he did today, he was without the ball also an important part of our game plan. Yes, these are the ones that score the goals, but if you watch the goals one more time back — and that's definitely what I am going to do — it mostly started off with centre-backs or full-backs. Every lead-up to a goal was, I think, multiple passes. So, it's not only the ones that score; it's also the ones that help to create.

You know, just as well as I know because I've won the league once, how hard it is to win it. You have to keep on going, keep on going. Every three days you have to be on top of your game every minute of the game. That's why it is so hard to win it because it's not always easy to show up every three or four days.'

Post-match notes

Mo Salah reached 229 Liverpool goals to go fourth, ahead of Billy Liddell, on the club's all-time list as the Reds won to ensure they remain top at Christmas.

December 2024

v Leicester City
Thursday, December 26, 8pm

'I HAVE LEARNED VERY QUICKLY WHY OUR FANS HAVE BEEN REGARDED ALL AROUND THE WORLD AS SPECIAL'

Premier League

Good evening and welcome to Anfield for our Premier League fixture against Leicester City.

For those of you who are reading this programme, the likelihood is that attending games over the Christmas period is not a new thing for you. I know how strong and important this tradition is in England, and although it will be different for me and some of my staff, we are all very much excited to be a part of it.

My only experience of this tradition previously was as a football fan in Holland because during the winter break I would always look forward to watching Premier League games on television. Now I will be involved as a participant, and I very much want to make the most of the opportunities that this brings, particularly as there are so many points at stake in such a short space of time.

Publication deadlines mean that these notes had to be completed before our away fixture at Tottenham Hotspur had taken place, but regardless of the outcome of that, my message would be pretty much the same — that is, that whether we have gained points or lost points on those around us, we will need a positive result today.

We are still just about in the first half of the season, but we are getting close to the point where everyone will have played half of their fixtures, and that is a moment when we will have a clearer idea of where we are all at.

This is why I have consistently said that judgements before this stage are not a true representation. It is only when each team has played one another and the fluctuations of form and fortune have evened themselves out that we will start to have a better understanding of how we are all performing.

For this reason – and many others besides – I want to finish this first half of the campaign as strongly as we possibly can. No prizes will be given out during this period, but as with the Champions League group, the longer you can be in and around the top positions, the stronger a platform you can give yourself to build going forward.

Of course, I would not be so naïve to believe that other clubs do not have the exact same objective no matter where they are in the table. Leicester will see this spell as a chance to push themselves up the table, and for this reason they will come to Anfield looking to make life as difficult as they possibly can for us.

I also know from experience how tough it can be playing against Ruud van Nistelrooy's teams, and my expectation is that Leicester will increasingly start to play in his image the longer they get to work with him. This adds to the challenge that we will face today, but as with every other challenge we have faced already this season, it is one that we should look forward to.

Finally, I would like to take this opportunity to wish all of our supporters a Happy Christmas. I have still only been at Liverpool for six months or so, but in that short space of time I have learned very quickly why our fans are regarded all around the world as being very special.

The support that you have given me, my staff, and the players is a big part of what we do and what we are trying to do. Obviously this applies most of all in the stadium on match days, but there have also been other ways that we have felt your support even when we are not at Anfield, so it is very important for me that you know how much this is appreciated.

I hope that you have enjoyed the football that the team has played so far, and you have my word that we will keep on working as hard as we possibly can to keep on improving. There is a lot of football still to be played, so hopefully the second half of the season can be as good – if not even better – than the first half.

On a personal note, I would also like to wish you and your loved ones what I wish for myself and my loved ones as we approach every New Year; that is, good health and good times.

Liverpool 3 Leicester City 1

Goals: Gakpo (45+1), Jones (49), Salah (82)

Line-up (4-2-3-1): Alisson, Alexander-Arnold, Gomez, Van Dijk (c), Robertson (Tsimikas 86), Gravenberch (Endo 87), Mac Allister (Elliott 90+2), Gakpo, Jones (Szoboszlai 78), Salah, Nunez (Jota 78). Subs not used: Kelleher, Quansah, Diaz, Chiesa

Arne's post-match reaction: 'First of all, it's important to win a game, and I think we should win at home against Leicester, but

I had the same feeling against Fulham and Nottingham Forest, so you always have to do a lot, especially in the Premier League, to win a game. And that was also [the case] today, because we went 1-0 down. The league table is something, of course, we are aware of, but we also understand how many games there are still to play.

I was happy with the first-half performance; I was happy with the start. There was only one minute I wasn't happy with, and that was the minute we conceded a goal. That was, I think, the only thing we didn't do well during the first half. We created from the start our chances, we threatened them a lot, brought a lot of balls into the box where we arrived with many players – I saw Robbo [Andy Robertson] many times in front of goal. So, I could not have asked for that much more. But I think it was crucial to score the 1-1 just before half-time because that lifted us up, and you could see that immediately in the second half, where we just kept on going with what we did. It was not only helpful for us, but I think it also worked the opposite way for Leicester; they felt like, 'Okay, now it's going to be tough.'

Post-match notes

Liverpool came from behind to record victory and make it 22 games unbeaten in all competitions. This match was the last of 28 at Anfield in 2024, the Reds winning 23 of them and scoring 74 goals in total.

Arne Slot

Sunday, December 29th, 5.15pm
Premier League
West Ham United 0 Liverpool 5

Goals: Diaz (30), Gakpo (40), Salah (44), Alexander-Arnold (54),
Jota (84)

Line-up (4-2-3-1): Alisson, Alexander-Arnold, Gomez (Quansah, 37),
Van Dijk (c), Robertson (Tsimikas 74), Gravenberch (Endo 57),
Mac Allister, Gakpo (Jota 58), Jones (Elliott 74), Salah, Diaz.
Subs not used: Kelleher, Danns, McConnell, Nunez

Arne's post-match reaction: 'If you only rely on one player when it comes to goals, that is mostly not really helpful, although it's also nice to have one that scores a lot. But then to see that others score goals and threatening the other goal as well is pleasing to see. It's not only the one that scores the goal; I think the lead-up towards the goal is also very positive from our point of view.

This is the way I would like to see us play an away game. I think it's always, especially in the Premier League, the defence come with a lot. There's a lot of fans in every stadium we play. The stadium is always sold out if Liverpool comes. They don't need much to cheer for if Liverpool comes because if they have an attack or a corner kick, the fans are already cheering, so then you have to kill that momentum as much as you can and not give away anything. I think there were only two, three, or four minutes where Curtis [Jones] lost the ball, Mo [Salah] lost the ball, and then we conceded a corner where the fans were a bit behind West Ham. For the rest, I think because we were so dominant we could manage West Ham but also the crowd.

I think the level you reach during the game always has to do with the team you face as well. West Ham has done really well before we faced them today. They were in a good mood, but normally West Ham doesn't compete for winning the league. I think you have to always take this into account. If you look at how happy you are with a performance, away games are always difficult in the Premier League. Especially here, I think last season it was 2-2, if I remember correctly. It's not an easy place to go to, so then to perform the way we did is pleasing to see.

Maybe we are a bit better, but it's not like we've increased enormously. What we did increase is scoring goals. There were games where we could've scored many more goals, but we didn't because we missed a few chances. Even today I think it was at half-time 3-0, but after 10 or 15 minutes we could've scored three easily with the quality we have. The good thing is that in the last weeks when the opponent had a chance, it was a goal [but] today they hit the bar and the post.'

Post-match notes

Mo Salah scored his 20th goal of an incredible season as the Reds made it 11 goals in two visits to London in the space of a week.

JAN

2025

Another eight-game month included a couple of insignificant defeats, FA Cup progress and eight points out of 12 in the league, including delirious scenes following a record-breaking win at Brentford

Coming up:
5th: Manchester United (PL) H
8th: Tottenham Hotspur (CC) A
11th: Accrington Stanley (FA) H
14th: Nottingham Forest (PL) A
18th: Brentford (PL) A
21st: Lille (CL) H
25th: Ipswich (PL) H
29th: PSV Eindhoven (CL) A

v Manchester United
Sunday, January 5th, 4.30pm

'MORE OFTEN THAN NOT, TIME IS NEEDED TO BUILD SOMETHING MEANINGFUL'

Premier League

Good afternoon and welcome to Anfield for our Premier League fixture against Manchester United.

As this is our first game of 2025, I would like to wish all of our supporters a Happy New Year. I am sure all of you have ambitions for the next 12 months – some of which we probably share – so I hope as many of them are realised as possible.

I was only at Liverpool for the second half of 2024, but I already know what a wonderful club this is with fans who give us incredible backing wherever we play, so I would like to take this opportunity to thank you for that.

We have done a lot of travelling of late to Southampton, to Tottenham, and to West Ham, and a constant feature has been the noise from the away end. Again, this is not something that any of us take for granted, which is why I want to bring extra attention to it.

We will need similar backing today, of course. The rivalry between Liverpool and United is one that people all around the world are aware of, and the main reasons for that are the history and success of the two clubs involved and the quality of the contests that take place between them.

The temptation for some will be to be drawn to the league table and to draw conclusions about what could happen today based solely on that. For me, this could only ever be a mistake. Even with my extremely limited knowledge of this fixture as a participant, I know full well that this is a game which comes down to performance on the day and not points on the board beforehand.

This is not to say I do not recognise that United have been in a tough moment of late. Their results have not been what they would want and this is something that everyone at their club will want to put right. I would imagine they will feel that there would be no better place to start this process than at Anfield.

United are historically a club which plans and invests to be successful. It was exactly the same during my first summer in the Premier League when they once again underlined their ambition in the transfer market to add to a squad which already had a lot of quality. The problem is we live in an era in which the expectation is that success should always follow immediately, but the reality is that, more often than not, time is needed to build something meaningful.

I would like to welcome Ruben Amorim, his players and staff, and the supporters of Manchester United to Anfield. I would also like to extend my best wishes for the New Year to all of you, even though it is clear that the rivalry between our clubs means we cannot share the same ambitions!

I have said since the start of the season that the halfway point in the campaign is a good moment to better understand the Premier League table and the possible direction that the clubs are heading in. We will reach that point after today's game – although it still will not be a totally true reflection, as the recent postponement at Everton means we have not been able to face every team – so the best way for us to get there would be with another positive result.

Whatever happens, though, there will be so much football still to be played. With 19 games to go and 57 points to play for, the halfway mark will only be a platform. It will not guarantee anything no matter what interpretations and conclusions people might want to draw. The truth is that while the hard work might not start now because it began last summer, it definitely does not become any easier now.

There are a lot of challenges still ahead – starting with today's against one of our biggest rivals – and as ever we will face them together.

Liverpool 2 Manchester United 2

Goals: Gakpo (59), Salah (70, pen)

Line-up (4-2-3-1): Alisson, Alexander-Arnold (Bradley, 86), Konate, Van Dijk (c), Robertson, Gravenberch, Mac Allister, Gakpo (Elliott, 86), Jones (Jota 61), Salah, Diaz (Nunez 60). Subs not used: Kelleher, Chiesa, Quansah, Tsimikas, Endo

Arne's post-match reaction: 'Of course, it feels for us as two points dropped. I think many people, what stays in their head for a long time is what happens in the end, and that was a big chance for [Harry] Maguire, of course. But what we tend to forget is two minutes before, Virgil [van Dijk] had maybe such a big chance as he had to make it 3-2 for us. In the end, it was a difficult game. A bit similar to maybe the Nottingham Forest game, where the playing style of both teams was quite similar. Defending in a low block with a lot of bodies, and if they had the ball, not the risk of build-up but play it long. Every free-kick they got somewhere in and around their own half or our half, they brought it in, so that was a bit similar to Forest. That is not always easy, then, to play against that style of football, and that's what showed against Forest, and it showed again today. Especially if they have such good quality players that can defend so well, then it is not so easy to play it through that low block that they had.

It's not so easy to take control if the other team plays every ball into your last line; then the ball is constantly in the air and there's constantly duels. That is, I think, what makes it difficult. We couldn't control it completely because every time we had control, we had a shot on target; Onana put the ball on the ground and hit it long towards our half. Of course, we had to do much better in the two goals we conceded, but that's what every manager says.'

Post-match notes

Mo Salah went level with Thierry Henry on 175 Premier League goals (eighth on the all-time list) but the Reds could only manage a draw.

Wednesday, January 8th, 8pm
Carabao Cup semi-final first leg
Tottenham Hotspur 1 Liverpool 0

Line-up (4-2-3-1): Alisson, Bradley (Alexander-Arnold 60), Quansah (Endo 30), Van Dijk (c), Tsimikas, Gravenberch, Mac Allister (Konate 80), Gakpo (Diaz 60), Jones, Salah, Jota (Nunez 60). Subs not used: Kelleher, Chiesa, Elliott, Robertson

Arne's post-match reaction: 'I never felt we were going to lose this game. Especially not after the first 15 to 20 minutes because I did feel Spurs started the game better than us. But after that, in my opinion, we had most of the game control, played most of the game in their half, had much more ball possession, and then a moment like this — if you go down to 10 for a few seconds against a team that can play good football, like Tottenham can, it's far from ideal.

[About the incident when Bergvall could have received a second yellow card just before the goal] I don't think there is any debate. They say he [Bergvall] didn't stop the counter-attack. I think every manager would prefer if the tackle were being made now 40 yards away from our goalkeeper — I don't think you really stop a counter-attack then — every manager would prefer to get a second yellow card for the other team than to finish that counter-attack with a player less to play that counter-attack with. If that is not a discussion, then the next discussion is if it was reckless enough, [so] just give advantage, then just come back and

say, 'Yeah, I thought the tackle was still too reckless.' So they still have to give a yellow.

In the VAR decision, he had to tell everyone what his decision was, and unfortunately, he didn't have to do this with this decision. Things happen. Very unlucky for us. The good thing for us is that if you ever have to lose a game, it's better that you lose one when there is still a second leg to be played. [It's a] far from ideal starting position for us because they have a really good team; probably some players will come back for the second leg. So, far from ideal to lose here, but if I ever have to lose, I prefer to lose if there's still a leg to be played. Then it would've been only this game.

When he didn't give the second yellow, nobody thought that it would have had such a big impact 30 seconds later. I think – I haven't asked him – but I am 99.9 percent sure I wasn't the only one who felt not the best [when the goal was scored]. I am 99.9 percent sure when Bergvall scored the referee was like, 'Is this really happening?' because he couldn't change it anymore. It was, for him, also far from ideal, I think – but that's why I say 99.9 because I couldn't look into his head, and he didn't have to tell what he felt.'

Post-match notes

Liverpool suffered only their second defeat of the Arne Slot era as Lucas Bergvall's controversial goal – after escaping a second yellow card – decided the first leg.

**v Accrington Stanley
Saturday, January 11th, 12.15pm**

'IF WE STAY TOGETHER WE CAN ONLY IMPROVE OUR CHANCES OF BEING SUCCESSFUL'

FA Cup third round

Good afternoon and welcome to Anfield for our FA Cup third-round tie against Accrington Stanley.

Even though the FA Cup is new to me as a participant, like everyone else who watched English football growing up, I do have "experience" of what makes it such a special competition, so I am looking forward to sampling it for the first time as a participant.

I am sure also that our opponents today will have similar excitement about this occasion, and I would like to welcome John Doolan and the players, staff, and supporters to Anfield. Accrington have earned their place in the third round with two very good wins against Rushall and Swindon Town, so we know they will be looking to do themselves justice once again.

For us, it is about looking to get back to winning ways. We have not done too much wrong over the last week, but we have not been able to get the results that we would have liked, and this is something that we need to respond to.

The defeat we suffered against Tottenham in midweek was disappointing because there was not really a period during the game when it felt likely that we might lose. I will not dwell on the reasons that were out of our control leading up to the decisive goal, but at the same time it would not make sense to ignore them altogether because they were so unusual and so significant.

But as I said immediately afterwards, if we have to lose a game, I would always prefer it to be one when there is a second leg to come. This does not make it okay to lose, but it does mean we still have an opportunity to put things right. That chance will not come for a while, but that does not mean we should not start the process straight away.

One of the positives that we can definitely take forward is the support we received from our fans. Seeing so many of you with us in London on a Wednesday night in early January was really impressive, particularly as we have had a lot of big away trips lately. It was also really important that you showed your support for Trent when he came onto the field in the second half. This, to me, is one of the things that makes the Liverpool fans so special.

There are always going to be times when things are not easy, but that makes it even more important that we stick together no matter what. This, to me, is what You'll Never Walk Alone means and this is why it is such an important song and also a saying at this club. If we stay together, we can only improve our chances of being successful.

On this note, I would like to pay tribute to everyone who worked so, so hard to ensure our recent fixture against Manchester United could take place. This would not have been possible without the efforts of the city council and its workforce, the local police, and our own staff, who all worked together in very challenging weather conditions to allow the match to happen.

In the aftermath of the game, the focus is inevitably on the result and the performances of the two teams, but we should also keep a focus on all of the many individuals who contribute on a match day and at other times during the week. Ideally, we would have liked to have rewarded them with a victory, but it was not to be. Regardless, the players and I have total appreciation for these kind of efforts.

For us, the focus now is to look for better performances and better results starting with a cup tie that history tells us has the potential to become very tricky if we do not perform. It is our responsibility to ensure that this does not happen.

Liverpool 4 Accrington Stanley 0

Goals: Jota (29), Alexander-Arnold (45), Danns (76), Chiesa (90)

Line-up (4-3-3): Kelleher, Alexander-Arnold (c) (Bradley 60), Quansah, Endo (Nyoni 79), Tsimikas, Jota, Morton (McConnell 60), Szoboszlai (Chiesa 46), Elliott, Nunez, Ngumoha (Danns 72).
Subs not used: Jaros, Diaz, Mac Allister, Robertson

Arne's post-match reaction: 'First of all, credit to them [for] the way they showed themselves here today. Of course, before the game starts you watch a few games of them and then you see, 'Ah, they're not afraid to press high, not afraid to play one-v-one.' But then you always wonder, will they do this at Anfield as well? But they definitely did. They were not afraid. Their playing style is also when the goalkeeper has the ball to play it long, so it is not that they stole this from the team we played last week; that's just their style. They showed up in a very positive way. For us, it was all about the players that haven't played that much yet, to give them playing time and give some playing time to a few youngsters.

I think he's [Ngumoha] been with us now for half a season. Every time when he comes training with us, we see what his qualities are. He can dominate one-v-one situations, he is very quick on his feet, he can change directions really fast. And I'm always happy if a player makes his debut that he shows what we see on the training ground as well, so the fans could see it. And I think the fans liked what they saw; you could feel this in the stadium in the first half already, and when I took him out, [from] the reaction of the fans, I think we could see they liked what they saw as well. So, special day for him – making your debut, win. He will sleep well tonight, I assume.

Rio was lucky that Federico [Chiesa] wasn't with us in the last two days – because he was sick – otherwise Federico would have started, of course. It's nice to make your debut, and if you have played for this club already, then you want to score your first goal, especially in front of your own fans. That's what he did now, so that's a good next step.'

Post-match notes

Rio Ngumoha, aged 16 years and 135 days, became Liverpool's second-youngest debutant. Only Jerome Sinclair was younger.

Tuesday, January 14th, 8pm
Premier League
Nottingham Forest 1 Liverpool 1

Goal: Jota (66)

Line-up (4-2-3-1): Alisson, Alexander-Arnold, Konate (Jota 65), Van Dijk (c), Robertson (Tsimikas 65), Gravenberch, Mac Allister, Gakpo, Szoboszlai, Salah, Diaz (Jones 75). Subs not used: Kelleher, Bradley, Endo, Chiesa, Quansah, Elliott

Arne's post-match reaction: 'I don't feel any pride in the substitution [bringing Jota and Tsimikas on immediately before they combined to score Liverpool's goal] because you make a substitution because you have a certain game plan for why you do this. In this situation, we brought an attacker in for a defender just to play even more attacking football than we already did because we needed a goal – or goals. Then scoring from set-pieces was not something I had in my mind when I brought the two of them in, but of course Jota can score a goal, and Kostas has a good set-piece.

I couldn't have asked for more today. I think most people talk about the second half – that they are really positive about the second half. If you ask me, I am also more positive about the second half than the first half, but if you play at this ground against this team, who are in such good form, hardly concedes a chance in every single game – and I have watched many of them back... so many counter-attack threats, almost every game they have counter-attack after counter-attack after counter-attack. We conceded only one counter-attack here today in 98 minutes of football of total domination. Unfortunately for us, that ball immediately went in.

Then in the second half, our ball possession also led to a lot of chances. You have to give credit, again, to Nottingham because the way they defend, they throw themselves in front of shots, in front of every cross, and then there is a goalkeeper that has an outstanding season this year and tonight again. Being 1-0 down over here, and it's so hard to score against this team, it's not what we wanted – we want to have three points, but in the end what I want, what the fans should want, and what the players should want is that they give it all they have.

I think you saw today again that I can still strengthen the team or impact the game with the substitutes I have on the bench. Not for the first time this season, these players have helped us, that I could bring in. If you look at today, like I said, I couldn't have asked for more.'

Post-match notes

No side has gained more points from losing positions than Liverpool in the Premier League this season (14). Diogo Jota scored with his first touch just 22 seconds after coming off the bench – Liverpool's joint-fastest substitute goal on record in a Premier League match.

Saturday, January 18th, 3pm
Premier League
Brentford 0 Liverpool 2

Goals: Nunez (90+1, 90+3)

*Line-up (4-2-3-1): Alisson, Alexander-Arnold, Konate, Van Dijk (c),
Tsimikas (Robertson 65), Gravenberch, Mac Allister (Jones 80), Gakpo
(Chiesa 87), Szoboszlai (Elliott 80), Salah, Diaz (Nunez 65).
Subs not used: Kelleher, Endo, Quansah, Bradley*

Arne's post-match reaction: 'Against [Manchester] United
everybody was focused on the [Harry] Maguire chance, but [in]
the seven minutes before we had three open chances. So many
times in recent weeks – against Tottenham as well – we missed
a lot of chances; against [Nottingham] Forest we missed a lot.
So, it would have been a bit surprising if I felt, 'Okay, after all
these chances missed today, we will probably score in the last five
minutes.' But the players proved me wrong again.

I think Darwin [Nunez] is having a good season, where he scores
goals, he works very hard for the team, he assists. But he's in
competition with a lot of good players, so that's why he's not
every single game on the pitch. But I'm very happy with him –
not only because he scored today two goals but that, of course,
helps – but I'm very happy with the other performances he put in
for us as well.

The first one was a long build-up; the second one was a counter-attack. He can, of course, score his goals against a low block because he's a striker, and he's a threat in crosses as well. Immediately after he came on, he had quite a good chance when Robbo [Robertson] crossed it in. But if it's about strikers or if it's about the team, if we would not have scored today in the last five minutes, then the headlines would have been Liverpool drops points again, and no-one would have told you [about] 37 shots on [goal]. What a display. How many teams were able against Brentford to have 37 shots on [goal] during a game? And now because of us scoring two, there is probably a bit of emphasis on that fact as well.

So, this is the industry we work in. As a manager, the team, the players, we all accept this, and we all understand that there is a lot of focus if it doesn't go well and not as much on the fact if you have a great performance. We are in an industry where it's about winning and losing – and not about if you play beautiful football. People only enjoy beautiful football if you win. And otherwise, there's no focus at all on the performance.'

Post-match notes

Darwin Nunez's late double sealed the win and made him the second-highest scoring Premier League substitute since his debut in the 2022-23 season with seven goals (Jhon Duran has eight in that time). Liverpool's 37 shots is the most ever recorded by an away side in a Premier League match.

v Lille
Tuesday, January 21st, 8pm

'WE ARE MASTERS OF OUR OWN DESTINY SO WE SHOULD MAKE THE MOST OF THIS'

Champions League group phase

Good evening and welcome to Anfield for the second to last fixture of our Champions League group campaign against Lille.

A lot has been said about what we have done in the competition up to now, but while a lot of the compliments have been deserved, we are well aware that there is still work to be done if we are to reach the knockout stage.

There are various possibilities over the last two rounds of fixtures that would allow us to achieve this objective, but the most important one involves what we do. As things stand, we are masters of our own destiny, so we should make the most of this by doing everything possible to get the result that we need to guarantee progress.

For this to happen tonight, another strong performance will be required. Lille have already shown their quality in the Champions League this season and have their own objectives for qualification, having recorded victories against Sturm Graz, Bologna, Atletico Madrid, and Real Madrid.

Those two wins against the big Madrid clubs tell us everything we need to know about what Lille are capable of. Clearly, they are very strong opponents who are more than worthy of our respect, and it is on this basis that I would like to welcome Bruno Génésio, his staff, players, and supporters of Lille to Anfield.

No doubt that they will be looking for a special night,

so we must do everything that we can to stop this from happening. Of course our best chance of doing this rests on maintaining – and wherever possible, improving – our recent performance levels, which have been really good even though we have not always secured the results that we have deserved.

This did not apply on Saturday, of course. Against Brentford we were clearly the better side, dominating almost all of the game, and even though we had to wait until the very end to secure the points, no one who was present could claim we were not deserved winners.

At the same time, it is also true that we came close to dropping points, and because we always challenge ourselves to improve, we have to recognise that this was not a position that we needed to find ourselves in. From the possession we had, situations we generated, and chances we created, the outcome should have been clear long before Darwin Nunez's late goals.

This is an area in which we will look to be better. Winning games is never easy, especially in the Premier League or the Champions League where the standard is so, so high, but taking opportunities when they come can make it a little bit easier to win.

At the same time, even though the recent period has been one where it has been more difficult for us to convert chances into goals, our performance levels have been very consistent, and we are definitely looking for this to continue.

It is hard to think of a game so far where we have stolen the points. Maybe Chelsea in the Premier League was one where we got more than we deserved, but even then the outcome was not unfair. In the majority of fixtures, we have secured victories because we have earned them.

Again, we are looking to maintain this, as it is the best route towards continuing the season in a way that we would like. This will not be easy, though, especially as the challenges are only going to get bigger, and this makes it even more important that we take nothing for granted and keep on working and building together.

Liverpool 2 Lille 1

Goals: Salah (34), Elliott (67)

Line-up (4-3-3): Alisson, Bradley (Alexander-Arnold 86), Quansah, Van Dijk, Tsimikas, Jones (Elliott 46), Szoboszlai (Endo 63), Gravenberch (Mac Allister 46), Salah, Nunez, Diaz (Chiesa 75).
Subs not used: Jaros, Kelleher, Danns, Morton, Robertson, Konate, Gakpo

Arne's post-match reaction: 'Now we are in a new format where some teams are high in the league table because they had a lucky draw, or some teams are low because they had a very difficult draw. It's far-off to say that it is an advantage to be No.1 or No.2. We still don't know yet if that's an advantage or not. You might be lucky; you might be very unlucky, and ending up as No.8 means that maybe you are lucky. So, for me, it doesn't tell me anything; what for me is the most important thing for tonight is that we've managed to skip a round, and that is definitely worth a bit.

What maybe today asked a bit more from them is that they had to be patient because the reason why Lille has done so well – 21 games unbeaten and the teams they've beaten in the Champions League – is how disciplined they are.

We were not starting to force [anything] because they are really compact and defended really well. We didn't force a pass; we just kept the ball for as long as we could. The only thing I wasn't happy about is that, not for the first time in recent weeks, it was one chance for the other team and a goal, but that's maybe a phase of the season we are in at the moment.

Special is, I think, the word that describes most of Mo's [Salah] performances at this club the best. Maybe there are even better words to use, but he's been outstanding for this club for so many years, and still he does [it]. Today [it was] a great goal. If Mo goes on a one-v-one, there's a serious chance that he is going to score, but this goal we scored probably tells you a lot about why we are doing so well, because the work rate from the players that won the ball back before Curtis [Jones] gave a great pass towards Mo – that tells you why we're doing so well.'

Post-match notes

Liverpool ensured progress to the Champions League knockout phase as Mo_Salah scored his 50th goal in European competition for the Reds.

v Ipswich Town
Saturday, January 25th, 3pm

'IT IS OUR JOB TO GIVE YOU THE OPPORTUNITY TO DREAM'

Premier League

Good afternoon and welcome to Anfield for our Premier League fixture against Ipswich Town.

Before looking ahead to today's game, I would like to congratulate everyone at Liverpool FC for qualifying for the knockout stages of the Champions League with one round of fixtures still to go.

Being Liverpool means it is not out of the ordinary to reach this level, but this does not mean it should be taken for granted. There are so many elements that need to come together on and off the pitch for this kind of achievement to even be a possibility, and it makes sense that we should recognise that fact.

At the same time, we know that this is just a staging point. We do not want to stop here. We want to carry on with the journey to see where it can take us, and this means the hard work that got us this far has to continue.

I am sure these are exciting times for our supporters, and that pleases me as much as anything because it is our job to give you the opportunity to dream but, again – and I cannot say this enough – everything we have done so far in the Champions League and also in the Premier League represents only the first half of the season. There is so much still to do.

This isn't to be negative. It is just the reality. Yes, we should be aware of how far we have come, but we also need to be just as aware of how far we still need to go. If we can do both of these things, taking learnings with us along the way while hopefully continuing to develop as a team, then our chances of being successful will only improve.

The positive on this front is that this has been one of our strengths throughout the season so far. It started in our opening fixture of the campaign against today's opponents when Ipswich gave us a really difficult first half, but we managed the situation much better in the second half and were ultimately able to show our quality.

This was definitely a game which underlined the saying that there are no easy fixtures in the Premier League. Ipswich made such a fight of it and made it so difficult for us that we had to search within ourselves to find the answers.

Ultimately, we were able to do so, but we should not expect today's game to be any less challenging, particularly as Ipswich have improved and become more experienced at this level since the first weekend of the season.

I would like to welcome Kieran McKenna, his staff, and the players and supporters of Ipswich to Anfield. I know that going into this game there will be some focus on Ipswich's last game, but we will not make the mistake of thinking that result is representative of their season because it is actually the opposite, and their competitiveness is clear.

We also will not use the league table as a gauge of how this game will be. I have said many times that where the English league is different to the league in Holland is that it is not so easy to predict how matches will go based on placings in the table.

Up to now we have had difficult games against Wolves, Ipswich, Leicester City, and Southampton, and they are the teams in the bottom four. With this experience and knowledge, we should definitely expect today's test to be no different, so it is up to us to recognise the challenge and rise to it.

Liverpool 4 Ipswich Town 1

Goals: Szoboszlai (11), Salah (35), Gakpo (44, 65)

Line-up (4-2-3-1): Alisson, Alexander-Arnold, Konate, Van Dijk (c), Robertson, Gravenberch (Endo 68), Mac Allister (Danns 80), Gakpo (Nunez 68), Szoboszlai (Elliott 68), Salah, Diaz (Chiesa 86).
Subs not used: Kelleher, Tsimikas, Quansah, Bradley

Arne's post-match reaction: 'It's been a few times now that we played a home game that we conceded a goal in the start of the game, but I think today is the way you want to start the game: we were aggressive, dominant. For 85 minutes they have hardly been in our half, I think. It is a counter-attack threat with the wingers they have and with Delap, but we managed to control that so, so, so well because of the amount of work we have put in. In the end, we are all a bit disappointed with conceding [from] a corner – the first one this season – but for 85 minutes it was almost a perfect performance against a team that goes to such a low block. That's not always easy, then, but the way we did it for 85 minutes was really good. If you look at almost all the times we lost the ball, I saw a reaction of many players. That is what I mean with playing against a team with fast wingers, with a good No. 9, that goes to such a low block. It's so difficult to control the counter-attack and the only way to do so is what Mo [Salah] did [defensive work].

I think that's the development the team is in, because when we played Brentford, we had 37 shots, a record in the Premier League for an away team. And then because he [Szoboszlai] is involved in that team, he will probably take a few shots then as well. It is us, the players behind the ball, bringing our attacking players even more in promising positions than we did in the beginning of the season.

Then if you zoom in on Dom, I think at the beginning of the season he would have played that ball to Mo, which most of the time was a very good choice because Mo can definitely score a goal as well. And now he decided to go for the goal himself and scored the goal himself. Nice for him because, in my opinion, he is a bit underestimated. Not by me, but he doesn't always get the credits for the fact he is very important for this team, because his work rate is unbelievable.'

Post-match notes

Skipper Virgil van Dijk reached a milestone against Ipswich: 300 appearances for Liverpool with 209 wins against only 44 defeats.

Wednesday, January 29, 8pm
UEFA Champions League
PSV Eindhoven 3 Liverpool 2

Goals: Gakpo (28, pen), Elliott (40)

Line-up (4-3-3): Kelleher, Bradley, Quansah, Robertson (Nyoni 64), Tsimikas, Elliott, Endo, McConnell, Chiesa, Danns (Nallo 83), Gakpo (Morton 52). Subs not used: Jaros, Davies, Mabaya, Morrison, Norris, Kone-Doherty

Arne's post-match reaction: 'Like expected, I think, an eventful game with many goals. I think everybody expected that before the game, for two reasons maybe. One of the reasons I think [is] two managers who always want to press high and want to bring the ball out from the back. So sometimes you see then certain mistakes – but it's always eventful. And for the other reason, because both teams, maybe mainly ours, were not playing in the set-up that we usually do, so then you see in some moments that we defend in a way that probably is not expected if we play with all of our starters. But still in the end we were able to definitely make a game out of it, especially with all these youngsters on the pitch. So, 'eventful' would be my word to use.

We had quite a lot of players that were not used to playing so many minutes in the last six or seven months. So it's especially for them also important that they make these 90 minutes and *were able to keep competing. Okay, Jayden [Danns] couldn't manage to play the whole game, but Federico [Chiesa] in the end was still sprinting, trying to do his work. So positive.*

Yeah, it's cruel [the red card for Amara Nallo]. He has never played first-team football yet, and then to make your debut at Champions League level is probably the hardest way of making your debut. I think he misinterpreted the situation, and that is immediately a problem at this level or at Premier League level. So, it's a big moment for him to learn from. It is cruel, indeed. You think in a moment like this, 10 minutes before the end, 'Phwoar, I'm going to make my debut in the Champions League,' and a few minutes later you go off with a red card. That is always difficult. But a career mainly is not always positive; there are also negatives, and he has to fight very hard to make sure he will play a second Champions League game.

It is a good achievement to end up top of this league. It is so hard to judge a league table after eight games, let alone if all the teams play different opponents. It doesn't tell me much, to be honest, because some teams have faced easier opponents than others. It's always nice if there's a new format that you end up No.1, but it doesn't give us any assurances for the next round.'

Post-match notes

Liverpool ended the Champions League league phase in top spot despite this defeat. Amara Nallo was sent off on his Reds debut.

L.F.C.

FEB

2025

A strong test of their title mettle saw the Reds take in road trips to some of the Premier League's most daunting venues as the games came thick and fast, but an unbeaten run – including a win against the champions – proved they had what it takes

Coming up:
1st: Bournemouth (PL) A
6th: Tottenham Hotspur (CC) H
9th: Plymouth Argyle (PL) A
12th: Everton (PL) A
16th: Wolverhampton Wanderers (PL) H
19th: Aston Villa (PL) A
23rd: Manchester City (PL) A
26th: Newcastle United (PL) H

Saturday, February 1st, 3pm
Premier League
Bournemouth 0 Liverpool 2

Goals: Salah (30 pen, 75)

Line-up (4-2-3-1): Alisson, Alexander-Arnold (Bradley 70), Konate, Van Dijk (c), Robertson, Gravenberch, Mac Allister (Jones 61), Gakpo (Nunez 70), Szoboszlai, Salah (Endo 88), Diaz. Subs not used: Kelleher, Tsimikas, Quansah, Jota, Elliott

Arne's post-match reaction: 'I said before the game that after our home game when we were 3-0 up at half-time, the way they came at us in the second half, I already knew what a great mentality this team has and quality as well. From that moment onwards they've done so well in the league. They've picked up points against so many good teams, not by luck, but because they're intense. They have quality, and that's why we knew it was always going to be very hard, and if you want to win here, maybe you need a bit of luck as well because the margins are so small. Our penalty was just not offside, and their goal to make it 1-1 was just offside. They hit the post twice, we had our chances as well, but it was a close call for us to win this game.

Only a few of them have been as tough like this and that's what I told them before. In all the data when it comes to running, they are so high up on the list, so we knew that if we would've had any chance of a result over here, we at least had to compete with them in terms of running, fighting, playing the duels, and all these things. I think that's what the players did, and having Mo Salah definitely helps in a game like this.

If you want to win here against a team that is so competitive, then you need a team performance and work rate. That's what we have and you need some quality individuals that make the difference for you and that goal of Mo was absolute quality, and the saves Alisson made as well. But it was not only them; the way our centre-backs were defending again today was also impressive.

Almost every game feels like this [vital victory in the race to win the Premier League] for me. We've had so many of our games until the end exciting, and there were a few moments already this season where it felt that we're just not on the right side. All the points we've got until now, I think we deserved them.

What I want from them and what they want from each other is that they fight in every single game from the first until the last second to get the maximum result, and that's what the fans expect from them playing for this club. That's what we try to do in every single game, and it's also necessary if you want to have any chance of a result in this league.'

Post-match notes

Mo Salah's double moved him on to 178 Premier League goals, now sixth in the all-time list.

**v Tottenham Hotspur
Thursday, February 6th, 8pm**

'HOPEFULLY TONIGHT WE CAN TAKE ANOTHER STEP TO FULFILLING THE AMBITIONS WE HAVE'

Carabao Cup semi-final second leg

Good evening and welcome to Anfield for the second leg of our Carabao Cup semi-final second leg against Tottenham Hotspur.

The equation tonight is pretty simple – we need to overturn a 1-0 deficit from the first leg if we are to achieve our objective of reaching next month's final at Wembley in the knowledge that Spurs will have the same ambition.

When the prize is so big and two very good teams share the same aim, it usually guarantees a very competitive game of football, and this is exactly what we are expecting.

This is what we got at the Tottenham Hotspur Stadium at the start of January, so it makes sense that, if anything, the desire of everyone involved will only increase given how small the margins are and what is at stake.

Of course I was not at Liverpool the last time that the club reached a Wembley final in this competition last year, but I know how special that day was for the players, staff, and supporters. I have no doubt, given what happened on that occasion, that it is a day which will be spoken about for many years to come, but our job now is to look to create new memories.

For that to happen, we will need a big performance, and we will also need Anfield to do what it does best. I already have experience of what makes this stadium so special, but I am reliably informed that the atmosphere can be even better on nights like this, so hopefully that will be the case.

I would like to welcome Ange Postecoglou, his staff, and the players and supporters of Tottenham to Anfield. It will be the third time our clubs have met already this season, so we certainly know each other pretty well.

I said before the first leg that what happened in our Premier League fixture would have no bearing on that fixture, and it gave me no pleasure to be proven right. We were disappointed about a big decision that went against us, of course, but Spurs showed a reaction on the night and scored a good goal, which leaves us with it all to do tonight because now it is our turn to react.

This is why I was so pleased with our performance at Bournemouth at the weekend. Let me be clear, it was not perfect and – as is almost always true – there were definite areas for improvement. But in terms of effort, intensity, togetherness, and mentality, it was a real team performance, the kind of display that we are going to need to repeat tonight and also in the coming weeks and months.

I said afterwards that what I want from the players and what they want from each other is that they fight in every single game from the first until the last second to get the maximum result, and that's what the fans expect from them playing for this club. This is what we try to do in every single game, and it is also necessary if you want to have any chance of a result in this league or the cup competitions.

If we perform in this manner, we do not get any guarantees of success, but it does create the kind of possibilities and opportunities that could potentially lead to success. This is what we are all working for, so hopefully tonight we can take another step towards fulfilling the ambitions that we have and our supporters have. As ever, the best way of doing that is by staying together and giving everything we can for Liverpool.

Liverpool 4 Tottenham Hotspur 0
(4-1 on aggregate)

Goals: Gakpo (34), Salah (51, pen), Szoboszlai (75), Van Dijk (80)

*Line-up (4-2-3-1): Kelleher, Bradley, Konate, Van Dijk (c)
(Quansah 86), Robertson, Gravenberch, Jones (Mac Allister 72),
Gakpo (Diaz 82), Szoboszlai, Salah (Elliott 82), Nunez (Jota 72).
Subs not used: Jaros, Chiesa, Tsimikas, Endo*

Arne's post-match reaction: 'Our performance today was something that pleased me most. Reaching a final should always be special, even for this club. This club is used to playing finals, but still then we are working very hard every single day to try to improve players – and the players want to improve themselves every single day – but we are also in this business to play finals. We already know how difficult the final is going to be because we faced Newcastle already. But, [there are] many games to be played before this final, and this is where our focus should be at.

Tottenham are conceding goals because they have so many injury problems – that is probably the main reason why they are conceding goals – but they are always able to score goals as well and create a lot. For us to be so aggressive without the ball that it took them 80 minutes before they had their first shot on target, it doesn't tell you anything about Tottenham, but that should tell you a lot about our work rate without the ball. To play against a team that is so good in creating chances, only conceding one shot is a good accomplishment.

It was so intense. The players were ready for it, the fans were ready for it, and we all simply wanted one thing – and that was going through to the final.

For me, there are two reasons why we've become stronger. First of all, if you play more often together, you know better what is expected. So, the first time I tell them how to bring the ball out from the back against a seven, nine and 11 press, they were maybe like, 'Okay, this should be done.' But the more times you face them, the more it just becomes natural for you. That helps. Second of all, I believe in the fact that the more games you play, the stronger you become, the physically stronger you become. So, some people think you get tired, but as long as you manage it well, I think players will get stronger by playing a lot of games.'

Post-match notes

The Reds reached their 15th League Cup final where they would face Newcastle – the first time the clubs would meet in a major final since 1974.

Sunday, February 9th, 3pm
FA Cup fourth round
Plymouth Argyle 1 Liverpool 0

Line-up (4-3-3): Kelleher, McConnell, Gomez (c) (Mabaya 11, Nunez 58), Quansah, Tsimikas, Elliott, Endo, Nyoni (Kone-Doherty 76), Chiesa, Jota, Diaz. Subs not used: Jaros, Ngumoha, Jones, Nallo, Norris, Young

Arne's post-match reaction: 'The result is obvious; it's a big disappointment, and [with] the way we played [there] wasn't a lot to be happy about as well. The only thing I was happy about is that the boys kept on fighting for 100 minutes, and probably the best part of our game were the last 10 minutes. So, that tells you that they kept on fighting. But credit to them, a good game plan, they worked incredibly hard, and they got a penalty that was deserved because it was a clear penalty. But that had a lot of impact on the game, of course, because both teams hardly had any chances, and all of a sudden you get a penalty kick. Again, which was the correct decision, but they were 1-0 up and kept on fighting until the end. The goalkeeper made one or two good saves in the end, but we hardly created anything at all.'

Post-match notes

Arne Slot made 10 changes to his team as the Reds suffered their third away defeat of the season – though the losses at Tottenham and PSV had little consequence.

Wednesday, February 12th, 7.30pm
Premier League
Everton 2 Liverpool 2

Goals: Mac Allister (16), Salah (73)

Line-up (4-2-3-1): Alisson, Bradley (Jones 61), Konate, Van Dijk (c), Robertson (Tsimikas 69), Gravenberch (Alexander-Arnold 61), Mac Allister, Gakpo (Nunez 69), Szoboszlai, Salah, Diaz (Jota 88). Subs not used: Kelleher, Endo, Quansah, Elliott

Arne's post-match reaction: 'It felt immediately after the referee blew his whistle that we lost two points. During the whole 98 minutes I didn't feel constantly like we were the ones going to win the game. It felt like an equal game and that a draw would have been a fair result but with us leading after 97 minutes, we were quite close to winning so it felt as if we dropped two points. We would have loved to go nine points up, it would have been better than seven!

But I think we won a lot as well. What I mean by that is when I look at the togetherness of the team, together with the fans, how much they fought together to get the result over the line. We've been praised so many times this season about how well these players can play but they showed a different side of themselves against Everton.

In my opinion, they were also so much better than the year before (when Liverpool lost 2-0 at Goodison). They were mentally so, so strong during a game that was played in the most difficult circumstances for them.

To stay strong together, fight so hard to be so mentally strong, that gives me a lot of confidence for the upcoming 14 [Premier League] games. I already knew how well they can play but the togetherness shows me that we are a very difficult team to beat.

Two or one days before the game I showed some clips from last season (at Everton) and how we reacted in certain situations. It's an ongoing process but if you want to play at a top club like this you need more than quality; you need mentality. It's a combination of what players have inside them and also you try to address on a daily basis.

I like a lot that he [Curtis Jones] stands up for the team, but there are other ways for him to do that for the team and the fans. I will talk with him about that. The same for me; I should have acted differently after the game as well. But it's an emotional sport as well, and sometimes individuals make the wrong decision, and that's definitely what I did.'

Post-match notes

Arne Slot, his assistant Sipke Hulshoff, Curtis Jones and Everton's Abdoulaye Doucoure were shown red cards in the immediate aftermath of an eventful match — the final derby played at Goodison Park. The draw meant the clubs finished level on 41 wins apiece at Everton's old home.

v Wolverhampton Wanderers
Sunday, February 16th, 2pm

'THERE IS SO MUCH FOOTBALL TO BE PLAYED AND WE WON'T LOSE SIGHT OF THAT'

Premier League

Good afternoon and welcome to Anfield for our Premier League fixture against Wolverhampton Wanderers.

Wolves are a team who gave us a very testing afternoon when we met at Molineux earlier this season. The first 15-20 minutes in particular was a challenging period because they made it difficult for us to control the game, and we had to show a lot of patience and work really hard to come away with a positive result.

I think the way that game went surprised some people because we went into it on top of the Premier League with Wolves at the bottom, but I said at the time that they were clearly in a false position and that the quality they had meant they would not stay there.

This has turned out to be right, with Wolves now out of the relegation zone, having picked up a very impressive victory against Aston Villa recently. That result speaks for itself, and it is a clear indication that we should expect nothing but another tough game this afternoon.

I would like to welcome Vitor Pereira and the staff, players, and supporters of Wolves to Anfield. Vitor may be a fairly new manager to the Premier League, having replaced Gary O'Neil less than two months ago, but he has incredible experience, having worked in a number of leagues over the last twenty years. As with all managers, I am very much looking forward to meeting him and competing against his team.

It is a key part of the season for them, and of course

it is exactly the same for us. The particular challenge for us today is to respond to the Merseyside derby as positively as we can. Yes, we can be disappointed by coming as close as we did to getting a win in that game, but we have to channel this disappointment in the right way, which means the focus should be on producing an improved performance and nothing else.

Including today's fixture, we still have 14 league games left to play with 42 points at stake, which equates to just over one third of the season remaining. There is so much football to be played, and we cannot and will not lose sight of that. The big lesson of the Premier League is that in any given fixture it is possible for any team to take points from another team, which means we have to do everything we can to keep our standards high.

As well as playing another very important game, today is important for Liverpool FC for another reason, as we will celebrate the incredible work of the LFC Foundation as they celebrate their Community Day here at Anfield.

Of course the Foundation is still fairly new to me, but in the short time that I have been here I have learned a lot about the work that they do for the local community, and it is clear that it is very special.

Looking ahead, I am looking forward to working with them more in the future and meeting more of the inspirational people that they support through their programmes with events like today giving us the opportunity to make even more people aware of the work that they do.

Hopefully by doing this we can also help them continue to raise vital funds to allow them to help even more people. I am told they supported almost 130,000 people last season, and so it's clear to see the impact they are having across our communities.

A football club is about so much more than just the football; it's about community, togetherness, raising aspirations, and giving people hope, and that is something that the LFC Foundation are doing every day.

Liverpool 2 Wolverhampton Wanderers 1

Goals: Diaz (15), Salah (37, pen)

Line-up (4-2-3-1): Alisson, Alexander-Arnold (Bradley 64), Konate (Quansah 46), Van Dijk (c), Robertson, Gravenberch, Mac Allister, Szoboszlai, Diaz (Endo 71), Salah, Jota (Nunez 64). Subs not used: Kelleher, Elliott, Chiesa, McConnell, Tsimikas

Arne's post-match reaction: 'Clearly it was relief at the end, especially after what happened on Wednesday. Those last eight minutes, and especially the last minute where we conceded a goal, you are so frustrated because you know that moment can also have [an] impact for the next game or for the next games that are coming up. And I think you saw today after us conceding the 2-1 that maybe for the first time this season we were a bit, 'Ooh...'

Today, 2-0 up, we had to deal with thinking we scored the 3-0 – completely the correct decision that he disallowed it for offside. Thinking we were going to score the 3-0 with a penalty [for] Mo [Salah], again, in my opinion, the correct decision for the VAR to turn that decision over. And then immediately receiving the 2-1, that is mentally not easy – and that's why these wins are probably even more important than when we outplay Tottenham.

It's difficult to win a game of football. People always feel like, 'You've got Mo Salah, what are you talking about? He will always score for you a goal.' No, no, no. It's so difficult to win a game of football every three days after everything you go through in a season, so that's why this win is an important one.

Again, today you saw how vital players like Jarell [Quansah] – and Wata [Endo] also – are for this team. If you want to achieve something, of course you need the goals from Mo or from Lucho [Diaz] or from the others, but you also need these players that, if you depend on them, bring up performances like this.

For a large part I enjoyed the game, but I didn't enjoy the last 20 to 25 minutes.'

Post-match notes

The Reds have scored two or more goals in 17 successive matches at Anfield in all competitions – their joint-longest run of scoring two or more at home since joining the Football League in 1893 (also 17 from February to November 2019).

Wednesday, February 19th, 7.30pm
Premier League
Aston Villa 2 Liverpool 2

Goals: Salah (29), Alexander-Arnold (61)

Line-up (4-2-3-1): Alisson, Alexander-Arnold (Bradley 66, Quansah 89), Konate, Van Dijk (c), Robertson, Gravenberch, Mac Allister (Diaz 80), Szoboszlai, Jones, Salah, Jota (Nunez 66). Subs not used: Kelleher, Elliott, Chiesa, Tsimikas, Endo

Arne's post-match reaction: 'The only reason why we could be happy with a 2-2 is because they got the last chance of the game, maybe their third chance after scoring two. So, that could be the only reason that we would say, 'Okay, a point is good to take.' But for the rest, I think for everything else I am not happy with the 2-2. I wasn't happy at all being 2-1 down at half-time – that didn't reflect, in my opinion, the first half at all. But that's the thing in football – if you concede a set-piece things can change quite quickly.

What I saw was an unbelievable pass from Conor Bradley and what a power run from Dominik Szoboszlai, who made, in my opinion, the perfect choice to square it [as] from a one-v-one to the goalkeeper he made it an open-goal chance. Then Darwin [Nunez], of course, it was not the best leg [because] he is right-footed, of course, but it was still a big chance. Yeah, very unlucky, and I was hoping that he could have got another one because a player like him probably wouldn't miss two chances in a row, and he was very close afterwards when he went towards [Emiliano] Martinez again, but Martinez made a great sliding tackle to win the ball. I think we are all disappointed.

I think every game has its own story. In terms of performance we weren't brilliant at all at Everton but for obvious reasons we were very unlucky to come away with a draw over there. Today, I liked our performance a lot — much, much, much more than I liked our performance against Wolves — from what I like the most: playing the ball, bringing the ball out from the back, creating chances. I think if you go away at Villa, that's always a difficult fixture. If you start the season you say, 'Oh, Villa away, that's a difficult one, [Manchester] City away, that's a difficult one.' So performance-wise, not a dip at all today in my opinion.

And what we must not do, and have done a bit too often now, is that we don't get what we deserve, and if you look at all the chances, if you put them in a row from us and them, I think it's clear which team should have won this game.'

Post-match notes

Mo Salah became the first player in Premier League history to score and assist in 10 different games in one season. The forward is the first player to do so in one of Europe's big-five leagues since Lionel Messi in 2014-15 for Barcelona (11).

Sunday, February 23rd, 4.30pm
Premier League
Manchester City 0 Liverpool 2

Goals: Salah (14), Szoboszlai (37)

Line-up (4-2-2-2): Alisson, Alexander-Arnold (Quansah 90+2), Konate, Van Dijk (c), Robertson (Tsimikas 74), Gravenberch, Mac Allister, Salah (Elliott 90+1), Szoboszlai, Jones (Endo 73), Diaz (Gakpo 79). Subs not used: Kelleher, Chiesa, Nunez, Jota

Arne's post-match reaction: 'If you play away at the Etihad, if you win there, it is always a big win, no matter what the league table looks like. If you play away from home against a Pep [Guardiola] team, it is almost impossible to have more ball possession than his team has. We knew we had to defend a lot, and that's what we did really well, and then some good moments in the counter-attack led to us winning the game.

In my opinion, Villa away and City away are two very, very, very difficult games, so you can drop points over there. But we are in a good position, but we also know how hard it was for us to win against Wolves.

Now we play against Newcastle [United], and we played a 3-3 over there, which was, in my opinion, also a good result, although after 89 minutes we were 3-2 up, but we also experienced how difficult that one is. In every other league, I think a lead like this would be very comfortable – except for this one because in this league every single game gives you a lot of challenges; even Plymouth Argyle gave us a lot of challenges.

What we do know is that no-one saw us as a title contender when we started at the beginning of the season – and I think no-one in the world of football would have expected City not to be so close to the one that leads the league if they are not the one that leads the league. We all know why but again today you could see how difficult they are to play against.

Today we scored from a set-piece and that gives you such a boost for this game because, at that moment of time, it wasn't that we were dominating the game. It wasn't expected that we could score at any second, so yeah, set-pieces are vital.

I think all of them want to achieve something this season. But we know how hard it is. The boys have worked every single day really hard to be where they are now, and I hope and assume that they will keep doing that for three more months.'

Post-match notes

In Arne Slot's first season with the club, Liverpool have done the Premier League double over Manchester City for the first time since 2015-16 — Jürgen Klopp's first season in charge. Mo Salah's opener for Liverpool was his 16th away goal in the Premier League this season, equalling the record for most away goals in a single campaign (also 16 by Kevin Phillips in 1999-2000 and Harry Kane in 2022-23).

v Newcastle United
Wednesday, February 26th, 8.15pm

'THIS CLUB CHALLENGES THE PLAYERS AND STAFF TO DO EVERYTHING THEY CAN TO BE THE BEST'

Premier League

Good evening and welcome to Anfield for our Premier League fixture against Newcastle United.

Of course, this will be the second time this season that we have played Newcastle with the first being a game that I am sure neutrals will have a lot of fond memories of. That 3-3 draw was eventful to say the least – a fixture that we could have won having been in a losing position and one that we ultimately drew in disappointing circumstances.

Maybe now that the season is in its final months that result is looked upon more kindly than it was at the time with the league table taking more shape and Newcastle having demonstrated on a number of occasions just what a challenge they can be, particularly on home ground.

They were also backed by an incredibly passionate home crowd on the night, something that I am hoping can be replicated – and perhaps even bettered – at Anfield tonight. Not only would this help us as we play our fifth game in fifteen days, it would also be what I believe the team deserves given the effort they have put in and the results they have earned during such a testing period.

I have already heard a lot about what this stadium can be like for this fixture, especially in a night game, so I am hoping that it lives up to that reputation. When I first arrived here last summer I already knew the difference that Anfield can make but seeing it, hearing it and feeling it is a very different thing to knowing it and I cannot say strongly enough that the more this kind of atmosphere can be reached the better.

Outside of the club there will be a lot of focus on the league table and what different results could mean but this is not our world. Our focus is solely on doing the work and maintaining the focus that we know is an absolute necessity to give us the best possible chance of winning our next game.

I know there will be those who believe this is something that we just say but I can assure them it is not. The reality is that in a league as competitive as this one, looking beyond the next opponent or getting drawn into possibilities can only be a distraction. This is not a mistake that we should make.

Also, we should bear in mind that it was only last week after a couple of draws against Everton and Aston Villa and a tough, tough home game against Wolves that we were being questioned in some quarters. Our view on those results was different and that is why we also did not get drawn into the narratives that followed. It makes sense that the same applies even after what was admittedly an outstanding win away to Manchester City on Sunday.

The exception that I would make to this is our fans. We do not just want you to dream, we need you to dream. This is a big part of what makes this club so special because it challenges the players and the staff to do everything that we possibly can to be the best that we can be. But it is important that you know that for us to stand any chance of living up to those hopes it takes an incredible amount of hard work every single day. There can be no let up.

Finally, I would like to welcome Eddie Howe and the Newcastle players, staff and supporters to Anfield for tonight's fixture. We will, of course, meet again in the final of the Carabao Cup in a few weeks time and I would like to take this opportunity to congratulate them for reaching Wembley and when the time is right both clubs can look forward to that occasion.

For now, our focus is on tonight and tonight alone.

Liverpool 2 Newcastle United 0

Goals: Szoboszlai (11), Mac Allister (63)

Line-up (4-2-3-1): Alisson, Alexander-Arnold (Quansah 77), Konate, Van Dijk (c), Tsimikas, Gravenberch (Endo 77), Mac Allister (Jones 87), Diaz (Nunez 87), Salah, Szoboszlai, Jota (Gakpo 62).
Subs not used: Kelleher, Elliott, Chiesa, Robertson

Arne's post-match reaction: 'What impressed me most was that this was our fifth game in 15 days and the four before weren't the most simple ones. To show up the way we did tonight, hardly conceding a chance against a very good team like Newcastle, is a big compliment for the players [in] how they handled these five games in 15 days.

I'm very pleased for him [Dominik Szoboszlai] because he's the type of player that always looks for a teammate in a better position than him if he has a chance. That is also what you saw against Villa, when he played that ball square for Darwin [Nunez]. For him to be on the scoresheet now for a player that is as humble as he is when he gets a chance, but especially because of his unbelievable work rate and what he does for the team, he definitely deserves [it]. I think he was Man of the Match today. He deserves the credit he is getting at the moment.

If you wear the Liverpool shirt as a midfielder, you should score goals, maybe except for the No. 6 but a 10 or an eight should provide goals as well if needed. Not always it has been needed, and sometimes they provide the assist, but today we depended on goals from them as well, and they showed up.

It doesn't matter which day of the week it is or if he has played, he [Endo] always gives his best in every training session and, as a result of that, every time the team needs him he shows up. That's a big compliment for him, that he brings performances in like he did today.'

Post-match notes

Arne Slot began a two-match touchline ban but it failed to unsettle the Reds who went 13 points clear at the top of the Premier League.

L.F.C.

MAR

2025

A disappointing month saw the Reds exit the Champions League stage to one of the continent's best teams and lose a cup final, which made the task at hand clear: pour everything into a league campaign that could bring the best prize of all

Coming up:
5th: Paris Saint-Germain (CL) A
8th: Southampton (PL) H
11th: Paris Saint-Germain (CL) H
16th: Newcastle United (CC) Wembley

Wednesday, March 5th, 8pm
UEFA Champions League round of 16 first leg
Paris Saint-Germain 0 Liverpool 1

Goal: Elliott (87)

Line-up (4-2-3-1): Alisson, Alexander-Arnold, Konate, Van Dijk (c), Robertson, Gravenberch (Endo 79), Mac Allister, Salah (Elliott 86), Szoboszlai, Diaz (Jones 67), Jota (Nunez 67). Subs not used: Jaros, Kelleher, Chiesa, Quansah, McConnell, Nyoni, Tsimikas

Arne's post-match reaction: 'I think if we had a draw over here, we would have already been lucky; that's clear for everyone. I think they were the much better team today, especially in the first half; they had a lot of open chances – three or four big, big, big chances. In the second half they were still the better team, still had a lot of shots on target, but they were mainly from outside the box. But I knew before the game, and I saw again today, how much quality this team has.

We were lucky in the first half that the goal [Khvicha Kvaratskhelia's disallowed effort] was fractionally offside... And in the end, we were already in the game three, four, or five times. I felt like, 'We can hurt them in transition,' but we didn't. We waited until the last moment, and then we hurt them.

A big moment for him [Harvey Elliott]. I can understand that he is sometimes frustrated by the playing time he gets because he is a good player; he showed at Liverpool already that he is a good player, but he is in competition with players that I hardly take off. So, Dominik Szoboszlai is always the one that just keeps on going; he also scores goals, but he's so important for us with all the running he does. And yeah, Mo Salah I think is quite key for everyone as well. So, he has to do it with limited playing time but he just keeps on going.

I have to give him big compliments for that and also my staff because they keep working with him and every time come up with great exercises so he stays fit. But it wasn't only Harvey [Elliott], it was also the one who assisted, Darwin Nunez, who came from a difficult two games but was there again tonight.

It tells me that we are, of course, [with] a 1-0 win and if you have seen the game, it is a very good result for us., But we also felt the quality of Paris Saint-Germain, and I knew it before: 10 times in a row they scored goal after goal after goal [and have] incredible pace with the wingers. So, every underlying stat shows you that they are the best team in the Champions League – so, we in the league table won it, but they were, in the underlying stats, the best team, so I wasn't surprised they were so good. We're definitely going to need our fans in a week's time.'

Post-match notes

Alisson's heroics in goal laid the foundations for this victory; his nine saves were the most by a Liverpool stopper in a Champions League game since Opta started recording the data in 2003-04.

v Southampton
Saturday, March 8th, 3pm

'THIS IS AN EXCITING PERIOD AND IT IS ALSO A TESTING ONE'

Premier League

Good afternoon and welcome to Anfield for our Premier League fixture against Southampton.

This is a game that comes on the back of a very testing Champions League match away in Paris, and because of the quick turnaround, it is clear that we will have to dig deep to go again. This is not a complaint; it is just our reality.

We do not get to make excuses, nor do we want to. We just have to do whatever it takes to give ourselves the best possible chance of getting a positive result. Again, if you are a team that wants to go hard in the Premier League and the Champions League — which we are — this is an obligation.

It is clear, though, that given the efforts that the players put in on Wednesday night, we will need our supporters today. In football it is sometimes easy to look at the fixture list and predict when there will be a big atmosphere, but sometimes it is as much about the need and the moment. This, I would say, is definitely one of those occasions.

Southampton are a team who have given us a big test already this season. Our fixture at St Mary's was very tight, as the result demonstrated, and it was yet another occasion when the strength of the Premier League was shown because we were pushed all the way even if expectations outside of ourselves had been that it be a much more straightforward game.

That experience will help us today, but only if

we use the information in the right way. We should expect Southampton to fight every inch of the way once again. We should be prepared for them to look to take advantage of any weaknesses we might show. And we should know that they have the quality to cause problems for any opponent, as has been shown on many occasions this season, regardless of what the league table might say.

After today we know that we will not play another Premier League game for a few weeks, so the aim will be to sign off in a good way before we look forward to the second leg against PSG, the Carabao Cup final, and then the international break. This is an exciting period, and it is also a testing one, so we have to meet each challenge as it comes before moving on to the next one.

For this to happen we need to have total focus. It is clear that others will start to focus on what could happen during the rest of the season, but we cannot be part of this other than knowing that if we stick to our approach, our chances of being successful will not be harmed. After today we will have nine league games remaining, and although this might not seem like too many, it is just under one quarter of the season, which means there is a lot of football still to be played.

We should also be aware that we will need to show different qualities along the way. There will be times when our football speaks for itself, but there will also be occasions when we have to show a different side.

This is why I was so pleased with the character that we displayed against PSG, a team which demonstrated why it is one of the best in Europe by making us dig incredibly deep to get a result.

It may not have been our most deserved win of the season, to say the least, but it did underline once again how much our players are willing to give. This is such an important quality, and we will need to see it again and again in the coming weeks and months.

Finally, I would like to welcome Ivan Jurić, his staff, and the players of Southampton to Anfield. This will be the third time this season that the two clubs have met, and on the two previous occasions the only difference in the result has been one goal in our favour. This shows how difficult it always is to win at this level, but with the help of our supporters, we will be aiming for a similar outcome today.

Liverpool 3 Southampton 1

Goals: Nunez (51), Salah (55, 88, pen)

Line-up (4-3-3): Alisson, Alexander-Arnold (Quansah 90), Konate, Van Dijk (c), Tsimikas (Robertson 46), Gravenberch (Endo 81), Jones (Elliott 46), Szoboszlai (Mac Allister 46), Diaz, Nunez (Jota 68), Salah. Subs not used: Kelleher, Chiesa, McConnell

Arne's post-match reaction: 'I didn't give them compliments at half-time, I can tell you. Maybe it was because I was sitting up there instead of being at the line because I know from experience that when you watch a game over there, you always feel like, 'Maybe I can even play in this game.' But if you are then at the line it's always more tempo. But I don't think I was wrong this time if I said at half-time that energy levels were far, far, far too low. That is what had to change, and that's why we made three substitutions.

The first goal, if you look at Lucho [Luis Diaz], how he takes that one-v-one on, I don't think I can select a clip where that happened in the first half. In the second goal, Ryan Gravenberch pushed up all the way at the 18-yard line to win that ball, which led to the foul on Darwin [Nunez], whereas in the first half, every ball that fell out they could just pick up the ball and start to play. The energy in the stadium for the players and the fans in the second half was completely different than the first half.

When I look at the game against PSG, we need to go one step up in terms of intensity. But if I compare it with the game today, we need to go three, four, five, six, or seven steps up in terms of intensity if we want to have any chance of reaching the next round.'

Post-match notes

There were 58 points separating Liverpool — at the top — to rock-bottom Southampton before the game but the Saints took the lead before second-half goals saw Arne Slot's side recover to extend their advantage at the top to 16 points.

March 2025

v Paris Saint-Germain
Tuesday, March 11th, 8pm

'THE INTENSITY THAT PSG PRODUCED SET A STANDARD AND WE HAVE TO MEET THAT CHALLENGE'

Champions League round of 16 second leg

Good evening and welcome to Anfield for the second leg of our last-sixteen tie against Paris Saint-Germain in the UEFA Champions League.

Anyone who watched last week's first leg will know what is at stake tonight and also the quality of our opposition. This is why I have described this game as a final – if we want to win it, we are going to have to put absolutely everything on the line because nothing else will be good enough.

I have spoken a lot about PSG in the days since we played them, mainly because it is clear how impressed people were with their performance against us. While I share that level of admiration, we were in no way surprised. The work we had done in the build-up to the game in Paris indicated that PSG had been the best-performing team in Europe so far this season, and the way they played confirmed this.

That we were able to come away with a narrow victory was due to a number of factors – most notably an incredible display by our goalkeeper – and we could not have been happier with the result in circumstances that were so, so, testing. But at the same time, we know we will have to be much, much better tonight. The need for improvement could not be clearer.

The standards that we set ourselves are always high, which is why it is unacceptable when we fall below them. This happened in the first half of our game against Southampton on Saturday, and we saw how difficult any game can be if we do not show the football characteristics that others expect of us and we expect of ourselves. This cannot happen tonight.

The idea for tonight is that the energy levels we will play with will be much higher than they were in that first half. They will also be higher still than they were in the second half even though we produced a much better performance in that period. The intensity that PSG produced against us set a standard, and we have to meet that challenge. This means stepping up a number of levels.

I said last week that if you want to win any major trophy there is always going to be a game or two along the way when you need to be lucky, but at the same time, history tells us that relying on good fortune is not the best possible route to success. Ultimately, it is performance that has always mattered most and will always matter most, so while we would never turn down a lucky win, we know that playing our best football will always give us our best chance.

I would like to welcome Luis Enrique and the staff, players, and supporters of PSG to Anfield for tonight's game. Our two clubs shared an incredible spectacle in Paris last week, and I am sure it was a game that created a lot of interest in Europe, just as this one will. I said immediately afterwards that Luis has put together an incredible team, and that is testament to the work he has done since becoming manager less than two years ago.

Tonight, though, PSG will not just play against

Liverpool; they will also play against Anfield and against our fans. This is an advantage that we have had for many years, and it is one that we have to make the absolute most of. I asked our fans to turn up on Saturday, and the response was good, especially in the second half when energy levels on the pitch improved, but tonight we need it to be even better.

In the short time I have been here, we have already had a couple of wonderful European nights, and when those occasions come along, the atmosphere is as good as anywhere in the world. What I have learned since being here is that Anfield is at its very best when the noise does not stop. It isn't just the songs – although the more of them we can hear, the better – it is a constant noise that makes the stadium so difficult for our opponents to play in.

It feels like I have asked a lot of our supporters lately, but this is only because I know what you can deliver and what a huge difference it can make to us as a team. The aim tonight is simple – to produce the best Liverpool performance that we possibly can on and off the pitch.

Liverpool 0 Paris Saint-Germain 1
(1-1 on aggregate, PSG win 4-1 on penalties)

Line-up (4-2-3-1): Alisson, Alexander-Arnold (Quansah 73), Konate (Endo 111), Van Dijk, Robertson, Gravenberch, Mac Allister (Jones 90), Salah (Elliott 105), Szoboszlai, Diaz (Gakpo 102), Jota (Nunez 73). Subs not used: Kelleher, Jaros, Chiesa, McConnell, Tsimikas

Arne's post-match reaction: 'It was the best game of football I was ever involved in. I don't have the history like Liverpool as a manager, but [it was] two teams of an incredible level [at] an incredible intensity. The first 25 minutes... Okay, I also remember the first 25 minutes against Man City at home and the first 25 against [Real] Madrid, but this was unbelievable what we showed in the first 25. I looked at the scoreboard, and we were 1-0 down. Over 90 minutes I don't think we deserved to lose this game of football today. Over 180 minutes, maybe it was deserved that we went to overtime. In overtime I thought Paris Saint-Germain was a bit better than us in this half-hour, and then it comes down to penalties, and they scored four, us one, and we lost.

Of course it is a shock. Maybe it is not the moment to tell them [the players] now — and I didn't tell them as well — but I can say it here: last season we weren't involved in the Champions League, and two seasons ago Liverpool went out against Madrid after losing 5-2 at home. So, if — if, if — you have to go out then go out in the way like we did against one of the best teams in Europe, making such a fight out of it. I hope and think every fan around the world was hoping this game would just keep on going; it wouldn't stop because it was incredible. They in the end won, and for us, it is so, so, so unlucky if you are No.1 in the league table that you then face Paris Saint-Germain, which is one of the best teams in Europe, but that's the format we are in. We have to accept it and we will come back stronger next season.

I am feeling disappointed about being knocked out. I do feel in the end of the season, it does matter how we presented ourselves in Europe. I just said, we were not in the Champions League last season, and this season we really showed ourselves. We can be proud of what we did. We won seven games in a row, and then we played with our substitutes and lost against PSV. I think we played last week, not our best game, but today we saw a completely different Liverpool. We go out in a way that I think has impressed Europe.

It is something now to take into consideration about how much worth it is to end up first in the league table if you can face Paris Saint-Germain in the next round. It is what it is. Maybe I am [speaking] too soon now, but maybe it would be more fair that after the round in between, the one that wins the league table plays against the team that is lowest position after the teams have played. But that is also because we were so unlucky to play Paris Saint-Germain because we could have also gone to the other side of the draw. In the end, if you want to win the tournament, you have to beat teams like Paris Saint-Germain, and that's what we didn't do today after an incredible first 90 minutes of football from us.'

Post-match notes

The Reds were eliminated from a major European knockout tie for the first time ever after winning the first leg away from home. It was also the first time the Reds have lost a penalty shootout in the European Cup.

Sunday, March 16, 4.30pm
Carabao Cup final
Liverpool 1 Newcastle United 2

Goal: Chiesa (90+4)

Line-up (4-2-3-1): Kelleher, Quansah, Konate (Jones 57), Van Dijk, Robertson, Gravenberch (Chiesa 74), Mac Allister (Gakpo 67), Szoboszlai, Diaz (Elliott 74), Salah, Jota (Nunez 57).
Subs not used: Alisson, Tsimikas, Endo, McConnell

Arne's post-match reaction: 'Disappointing result, disappointing performance. So, completely different than I felt after the Paris Saint-Germain game. Losing twice in a row is something I think we do for the first time. But that probably also comes with going into the latter stages of a tournament, so facing Paris Saint-Germain and Newcastle in a final are two very good teams, both in their own styles. But very difficult teams to face, because we already knew from the game at St. James' Park how difficult it is to beat them. It was a tough week, but it was also a week where we extended our lead [in the Premier League] to 12 points from it being 10, so it wasn't all negative. But the last two were definitely not the way we wanted it to be.

The game was slow and not intense, so it's difficult to judge for me if we were physically ready. Mentally, that's always a difficult one. If you look at the result and the performance, you might feel it maybe did something to us, but I prefer to look at how the game went. And this game went exactly the way they wanted it to be: a fight with a lot of duels and a lot of duels through the air. And if we play 10 times a game of football through the air against them, they win it probably nine times because they are a stronger team through the air than us, which led to the first goal and the second goal because the second goal was also a header that they won at the second post that fell for Isak and led to the 2-0.

Players have 15 years to play football and they want to win every single trophy they are competing for. That's also what we want. But it was a game that went the way they wanted it to go. And they got just before half-time some extra energy with the goal, which they probably deserved after the first 45 minutes because they were threatening us more than we were threatening them.

We are one of the biggest clubs in the world, Liverpool. But it's not for the first time in their history, or in the last two seasons, that they've lost two games in a row. This is part of playing football, especially if one of them is when you face the best team in Europe at the moment, and the other one is facing Newcastle, which is a very strong team in England.'

Post-match notes

The 65th League Cup final went Newcastle's way as Eddie Howe's club won their first major trophy since 1969. Liverpool remain the most successful club in the competition's history with 10 wins.

![L.F.C. crest]

APR

2025

With just the Premier League left to concentrate on, 12 points out of 15 – some of them won in the most dramatic of fashions – would take Arne Slot's men to a conclusion that will live long in the memory of every fan who witnessed it

Coming up:
2nd: Everton (PL) H
6th: Fulham (PL) A
13th: West Ham United (PL) H
20th: Leicester City (PL) A
27th: Tottenham Hotspur (PL) H

v Everton
Wednesday, April 2nd, 8pm

'WE NEED TO HAVE A LASER FOCUS. THE ONLY THING THAT MATTERS IS THE HERE AND NOW'

Premier League

Good evening and welcome to Anfield for our Premier League fixture against Everton.

It feels like a long time since we last played a home league game, so hopefully the wait will only add to the sense of anticipation for what is always one of the biggest games of the season.

Without dwelling too much on everything that happened before the international break, it is clear that a couple of important results went against us in both the Champions League and the Carabao Cup. In each case we congratulate our opponents in the knowledge that we have to use our own sense of disappointment in a positive way – starting tonight.

We are now down to the final nine matches of a season in which the players, staff, and supporters have already delivered so much, and yet there is so much still to play for. The situation that we are in is the kind that we would all have wanted when our campaign began at Ipswich Town back in August, so now we must make the most of it.

This means remaining focused on ourselves and our own results, not becoming distracted by anything else, and reaching the standards that we know will be required in each and every game that we play.

I said before the break that it was a big positive that our advantage at the top of the table had increased, but at the same time we are all aware that these kind of leads are always likely to fluctuate, particularly in a league which is as competitive as the Premier League.

Of course this has been shown by tonight's opponents, with Everton being on a really good run and picking up some excellent results since the return of David Moyes. I would like to welcome David, his staff, and the players and supporters of Everton to Anfield in the knowledge that they will be coming to put up a really good fight just as they did at Goodison Park back in February.

That was my first experience of the Merseyside derby, and it was quite an occasion. I know that the atmosphere that night was added to by the fact that it was the last derby match to be played at Goodison, but I am hoping that the circumstances around this fixture and the possibilities that could be created by a positive result for us will see Anfield at its very best.

Because we know what Anfield can be like and what a huge difference it can make, it is inevitable that we would want it to be like this all the time. Maybe that is unrealistic, but it should always be our ambition on and off the pitch, knowing that the closer we can get to our very top level, the better our chances of success.

It was funny before the break because I was asked on many occasions about which game was the most important because we were still involved in three competitions, but my answer was always the same – the next one is the most important. I think maybe not everyone believed me, but it was and is absolutely true.

We need to have a laser focus. There can be no

looking ahead and definitely no looking back; the only thing that matters is the here and now.

The next game is the most important game. The next game is the Merseyside derby against Everton. We should put everything we have into this one and then move on to what comes next. If we do it this way – and that is absolutely non-negotiable – we will see where it takes us.

Liverpool 1 Everton 0

Goal: Jota (57)

Line-up (4-2-3-1): Kelleher, Jones, Konate, Van Dijk (c), Robertson, Gravenberch, Mac Allister, Diaz (Gakpo 86), Salah (Endo 90+3), Szoboszlai, Jota (Nunez 75). Subs not used: Jaros, Elliott, Chiesa, McConnell, Quansah, Tsimikas

Arne's post-match reaction: 'Hard-fought, definitely, but that was no surprise. Everton were nine games in a row unbeaten, hardly ever concede a goal, hardly ever concede a chance, defend with 10 players apart from Beto in and around their 18-yard box. With players like Tarkowski and Branthwaite, it is almost of no use to bring a cross in because they head every ball away. So, they are a team that is difficult to play against because they are also a threat on the counter-attack. Every throw-in they get and every free-kick they get against us, you have to defend that, and that's what makes it so difficult.

At Goodison Park we had ball possession, but we only had ball possession with our centre-backs and full-backs, and today only in the first half. I think if I say 10 or 15 times that Lucho Diaz was one-v-one against Jake O'Brien, I don't even think I exaggerate, but to have that is one thing, and to create a chance is another thing. That's why we have to be there so many times, so many times, so many times, and you're hoping that one time can then be enough – and it was with Diogo's [Jota] goal.

For the goal he [Jota] found just a bit of space, and he scored the goal, which was nice for him but nice for us – and by us, I mean his teammates, the staff, and the fans.

I don't want to comment about the situation [Tarkowski not receiving a red card] because so many people already commented on that, even people that are not liking Liverpool a lot, and they were all so clear and obvious what the decision should have been. There's no need for me to comment on that. Was I surprised? No.

I don't mind if they take 10 seconds or a minute. If you are a VAR and you think it's not a red card, then you can also say it in 10 seconds; you don't have to wait for me to look at it for a minute. It's a human being that makes a decision, so the referee makes a decision; a human being makes the decision over there. I don't mind if they take 10 seconds, or a minute, or two minutes, or three minutes. They should take the right decision.'

Post-match notes

This win meant the Reds had only lost once at home to Everton in 25 previous meetings. This was Liverpool's first 1-0 Premier League home win since May 2023.

Sunday, April 6th, 2pm
Premier League
Fulham 3 Liverpool 2

Goals: Mac Allister (14), Diaz (72)

Line-up (4-2-3-1): Kelleher, Jones, Konate (Bradley 67), Van Dijk (c), Robertson (Chiesa 82), Gravenberch, Mac Allister, Gakpo (Diaz 55), Salah, Szoboszlai (Elliott 55) Jota (Nunez 67). Subs not used: Jaros, Endo, Quansah, Tsimikas

Arne's post-match reaction: 'I saw some very good build-up situations, the way we positioned ourselves. So, it wasn't 45 minutes of disaster, but the errors we made, I think, are something we are not used to, and that's something different than playing poorly, in my opinion.

One of the reasons why we are in the position we are in is we don't make a lot of mistakes, and if we do, players try to make up for them. Now, this is also what we tried to do with the second goal, but, unfortunately, instead of the ball being deflected [and] going behind, it went into the goal.

This can happen, especially if you play a good team like Fulham. If you make mistakes, they have the quality to punish us. I think in the end [in the] second half we created so many chances that we could have made up for it. But we lacked time, especially in the end, because in the first 20 minutes of the second half it didn't feel to me as if we could score a goal. But in the last 20 to 25 minutes, I think it was clear for everyone that we could score the third. That's why actual playing time wasn't the most in the last 25 minutes.

I think there is no reason for us to be complacent. We are not No.1 at the moment because we win every game with a margin of three or four goals. I think everyone that has seen our games [knows] it takes us so much effort, so much hard work to win games of football, combined with quality, of course. The team that won the league in the last four seasons were already 3-0 up at half-time almost every single game they played.

That's not the way it is for us, so we are fully aware of the fact we have to compete for seven more games. We saw it on Wednesday when we played Everton; it was a close call. Today it was a close call, and many times we've been on the right side. Today we were on the wrong side, mainly because of the errors.

They showed great character in the second half, but not for the first time this season we had a difficult first half. It didn't happen a lot, but I can come up with Southampton at home, for example, where we played quite poorly. Normally we are able to make up for that because of the mentality of the team, how fit they are, the subs we can bring [on]. Today it wasn't enough.'

Post-match notes

The Reds' 26-match unbeaten run in the Premier League comes to an end.

**v West Ham United
Sunday, April 13th, 2pm**

'IT WOULD MAKE A BIG DIFFERENCE TO HAVE A DERBY-STYLE ATMOSPHERE'

Premier League

Good afternoon and welcome to Anfield for our Premier League fixture against West Ham United.

Our record this season has meant that there have not been too many occasions when we have needed to bounce back from a bad result, but that is exactly what we must do today.

What happened at Fulham last weekend was, of course, a disappointment. It was a game in which we caused ourselves problems with all three of our opponent's goals coming from situations that we should have dealt with better. This is something that we acknowledged straight away because the first step towards addressing problems is admitting that they exist.

At the same time, it is even more important that we do not lose sight of the bigger picture. This was only the second league game that we have lost this season, and given how competitive football is in the Premier League, that says a lot about not only our consistency but also about how we have dealt with different challenges.

Today is another challenge against a West Ham team which has come under new management since the last time we played back in December. The work of Graham Potter in this country is well known, and his career in general is the kind that deserves nothing but respect. I would like to welcome Graham, his staff, and the players and supporters of West Ham to Anfield for what everyone will expect to be a highly competitive game.

The result of our last meeting may be misleading in this regard. West Ham were not in their best moment at that particular time, and we were in a period when we were scoring a lot of goals. These elements combined gave extra emphasis to the difference between the two teams on the day. We know also that it was not so long ago that West Ham became one of the very few teams who have been to Arsenal and won, so we should – and we will – be prepared for yet another big test.

As anyone who reads these notes regularly will know, I always like to include a message to our supporters because you are so vital to everything that we do, but today I have two. The first is pretty normal, and that is we are going to need you to be at your best in the games we have remaining at Anfield this season.

The atmosphere in our last home fixture was very special, especially in the minutes after Diogo Jota scored the decisive goal. That, of course, was in a Merseyside derby, and I have been in football long enough to know that a local rivalry will always bring out the very best in fans. The situation we are in with just seven games to go, though, means it would make a big, big difference if we could have a derby-style atmosphere in all of our home matches.

Secondly, today we will pay our respects to the men, women, and children who died in the Hillsborough disaster ahead of Tuesday's 36th anniversary. This is a responsibility that everyone at the club takes extremely seriously, and despite still being relatively new to Liverpool FC, I am very much aware of the toll that the tragedy took on our supporters, both in terms of the disaster itself and the injustices that followed.

We also recognise that there will be many amongst us today who are survivors of Hillsborough or who lost loved ones on that day. Again, I want you to know that we will always stand with you, and we will never forget the 97 victims who were unlawfully killed. Not just this week as we commemorate the anniversary, but every single day. This is our duty to you as representatives of Liverpool Football Club.

Liverpool 2 West Ham United 1

Goals: Diaz (18), Van Dijk (89)

Line-up (4-2-3-1): Alisson, Bradley (Quansah 68), Konate, Van Dijk (c), Tsimikas (Robertson 60), Gravenberch, Mac Allister, Salah (Endo 85), Jones (Szoboszlai 68), Jota (Gakpo 60), Diaz. Subs not used: Kelleher, Jaros, Elliott, Chiesa

Arne's post-match reaction: 'It was a big relief. Ali [Becker] made sure that they didn't score earlier. They had multiple chances to score the 1-1 in the second half, and unfortunately they scored one, which they didn't score but we scored [with an own goal]. To be completely honest, I was expecting two minutes with three or four minutes of added time, but all of a sudden seven minutes were added on with no time-wasting at all from both teams, which was a bit of a surprise for me. But okay, it helped because we scored a goal just before the extra time, and, of course, that was a relief because, to me, it felt after West Ham scored and the way the second half went, it was maybe more that you could expect them scoring. But our fans and our players thought differently because from the moment they scored the 1-1, we started playing again, we started pressing again, the fans were really loud at that moment of time. Already the chance from Lucho [Diaz], some counter-press moments which led to the corner kick, and then we saved a big set-piece for a very important moment because in the modern game of football set-pieces are that important.

Two more wins [needed]. I think the first 32 games have shown us how difficult it is – not only for us but for every team in the Premier League – to win a game of football. So, the competition has never been as strong as it is this season. That's what makes it so hard to win a game of football. Everybody can say, 'You have to win two.' We still have to win two, so we should be completely focused on that. This week we should try to improve, improve, improve more and more to give ourselves a better chance of winning a game of football next week.'

Post-match notes

Arne brought up his half-century at the helm, and the success was the team's 36th win under the head coach, which is the most any Liverpool manager has ever registered in their opening 50 fixtures.

Arne Slot

Sunday, April 20th, 4.30pm
Premier League
Leicester City 0 Liverpool 1

Goal: Alexander-Arnold (76)

Line-up (4-2-3-1): Alisson, Bradley (Alexander-Arnold 71), Konate, Van Dijk (c), Tsimikas, Gravenberch, Mac Allister, Salah, Szoboszlai (Elliott 71), Gakpo (Jota 60), Diaz (Jones 90+4). Subs not used: Kelleher, Robertson, Quansah, Endo, Nunez

Arne's post-match reaction: 'I think every manager in the world would have brought Trent [Alexander-Arnold] in. There are no credits for me, but definitely for Trent because he has worked so hard for five-and-a-half weeks – including the medical staff that worked so hard with him to get him back in the squad as soon as he could. That's why we could use him today for [20] minutes, but I had to use him for 27 because of added time.

I think it meant a lot for everyone – for everyone who loves Liverpool. It is a big moment, and big players like to have big moments in their careers. Virgil [van Dijk] had one last week in a special moment; Mo [Salah] has had them many times this season already. Players with the quality of Trent, these players step up when you most need it. He did that when he came in against Newcastle [United], he did that in his second-half performance against Paris Saint-Germain, where I was just waiting for him to score a goal until the moment he had to go out with an injury. Now he is back, and he has had his moment. All nice, but still one to go.

It was another big moment for us to score from a set-piece, with us putting so much effort in for nine or 10 months now. It feels really good that in the moment we needed it most, although we needed it against Paris Saint-Germain as well when we headed it on the post from Jarell [Quansah]. Now, two big moments for us to score from a set-piece.

The only thing the fans want is us winning the league. After one league title in 35 years with them not being involved because of COVID. They were involved, but not as much as they probably wanted. Every moment that it happens, it would be special for them. [I am] definitely looking forward to next week because I assume that Arsenal, because they are such a good team, are able to win during the week. We probably have to do it ourselves, and the first chance we have is next week against Tottenham.

What I know from my time with Feyenoord is that of course there is a lot of noise and everybody is very excited, but at our training ground we are just focused on the training sessions we do and trying to prepare in the best possible way for Tottenham, a team that deserves our full attention.'

Post-match notes

The Reds moved to within one win of the title but the 1-0 victory confirmed Leicester City's relegation.

v Tottenham Hotspur
Sunday, April 27th, 4.30pm

'WHAT WE HAVE IS A WONDERFUL OPPORTUNITY THAT WE SHOULD GRAB WITH BOTH HANDS'

Premier League

Good afternoon and welcome to Anfield for our Premier League fixture against Tottenham Hotspur.

The overriding message today is very simple – we have a job to do. It is a job that everyone associated with Liverpool FC should be excited about because the possibilities it creates are there for all to see, but as with every other game we have played this season, hard work will be absolutely crucial.

So focusing on the job at hand is not just desirable; it is absolutely essential. On and off the pitch, our aim has to be to get as close as we possibly can to our A game. Reaching those standards will not be easy – it never is – but it needs to be the objective of everyone who is inside the stadium today.

I have spoken many times previously of admiration for Ange Postecoglou and the football that his teams play. My expectation is that his Tottenham Hotspur team will show their best levels ahead of their Europa League semi-final, and if they do this, we will definitely have to show ours.

That is the beauty of the Premier League. The standard is so, so high that each and every round of fixtures brings an obstacle that is so challenging that you have to give absolutely everything if you want to overcome it. Anyone who watched our most recent league games against West Ham United, Leicester City, Fulham, and Everton will not need telling this.

It is a league of small margins and big tests. Nothing

can ever be taken for granted, and if it is, the likelihood is that you will receive a painful reminder of what is required. Total focus is always required. Without it the possibility of winning diminishes whether you are facing a team from the top or one from nearer the bottom. For these reasons and many more, the Premier League is not only the best in European football, it is also the most competitive.

So what we have now and in the remaining weeks of the season is a wonderful opportunity that we should grasp with both hands. Finishing top of this league would be an incredible achievement, and having put ourselves in a position to do so we now need to finish the work that began all the way back in the summer of last year.

The effort that has gone into each and every training session and each and every game since then has been remarkable, but it has also been an absolute necessity. Imagine for a second if those standards had been dropped on only one or two occasions. I have no doubt that we would find ourselves in a different situation today if that had happened.

That it hasn't is testament to every single player, every single staff member, and every single supporter. The story of this season for us is that everyone has pushed each other on.

I could pay endless compliments to all involved, and hopefully the time for that will come, but the most important thing right now is that we all recognise that this would not be the time to stop.

To our supporters, this message is tinged with gratitude. Every time we have needed you so far this season, you have delivered. In our most testing moments you have lifted the team to a level that has helped us to win games that might have got away from us otherwise. There are so many good examples of this, but the most recent fixture at Anfield is probably one of the best, as it helped get us over the line against West Ham.

It must feel like I am always asking for things from you, but the reason for this is simple – like many at Liverpool before me, I have seen the difference that our crowd can and does make. This is why our players and our supporters have been able to create something special between them. Today we have an opportunity to do the same again. We should make the most of it.

Liverpool 5 Tottenham Hotspur 1

Goals: Diaz (16), Mac Allister (24), Gakpo (34), Salah (63), Udogie (69, OG)

Line-up (4-2-3-1): Alisson, Alexander-Arnold (Endo 76), Konate, Van Dijk (c), Robertson, Gravenberch, Mac Allister (Nunez 83), Salah, Szoboszlai (Jones 67), Gakpo (Jota 67), Diaz (Elliott 76). Subs not used: Kelleher, Quansah, Chiesa, Tsimikas

Arne's post-match reaction: 'I'm very, very happy, of course, but to a certain extent also [it feels] quite unreal because you work so hard for this moment to happen, and when it then does happen, it needs some time for you to truly feel it. But the fans were so happy that it didn't take us long, didn't take me long to understand what we've achieved together this season.

That is so, so special. The moment I knew I would become the new head coach over here, that's already a moment that you're so proud of — to be part of such a great football club. Then now to be part of the history of this football club is something I think I could only have dreamt of two, three, or four years ago. I don't know if it's funny or not, but I think four, five, or six years ago it was the first time when I was here when Pep Lijnders invited me — that was against Tottenham and I think they won that game 4-0 somewhere around Christmas time. We all know what happened around Tottenham one or two years ago, so now to win it against them is quite special. The [person] I was with was my sporting director at Cambuur Leeuwarden, where I worked back then; he showed me that we were visiting a match from the U21s where Trent [Alexander-Arnold] and Joe [Gomez] were involved in that game. So, a special day and not the first time I was here when we played Tottenham.

The only moment I was emotional today was when we arrived at the stadium — to see what it meant for the fans, what it meant for these people. For us to have a chance of winning, it felt really special, but immediately it also felt like, 'We still have to do it.' But I think everybody who was inside that bus felt that if the fans are with us, like they are, then it's impossible for us to lose this game of football. During the game, after the game, it's been

*incredible how the support of the fans were and how our players
played. Special to be part of this day.*

*I don't remember exactly what he [Liverpool owner John W.
Henry] said [to me], but it was special for them as well to be
part of this moment. For them to trust me to be in this position,
maybe now everybody says, 'That makes complete sense.' But the
moment they signed me, maybe not everyone was as convinced as
everyone is now. So, that tells you also what a special club this
is that they don't always go for maybe the most simple or obvious
choice – they make the choice that they think is best for the club.
It must be a special moment for them as well, the second time in
five years that they win the league. And now to do this in front of
our fans is special for everyone, including them.*

*I'm very proud. It's special to have them with me because my
family, all the families of the players, have to make sacrifices
if you do this job – not only this season, throughout your whole
career. Like you, everyone works really hard, but we're not
always home. Of course for me, my family was still in Holland,
so in moments it was hard for me but definitely for them as
well. And then now to win it, I think everybody feels that the
few sacrifices we've made were definitely worth it. And then it's
special that they can experience this moment as well.*

*[Jürgen Klopp helped] because of what he did before I even
arrived here. I think that is something not one manager ever did
before. So that is what definitely helped me. But apart from
that, he helped me even more by the team he left behind and the*

culture he left behind in that team. The quality the players have was obvious for everyone, but the culture of hard work — not only from the players but also from the staff members — has been incredible, and that is one of the reasons why we could achieve what we have achieved this season. For obvious reasons, I think it was a nice moment to thank him as well.

He was probably longer in his job than I am; he knew the club even better than I know it at the moment. But what I noticed from the first day I came in was that winning the league would be the most special trophy we could win. I think I felt that throughout the whole season. Although we were all very disappointed when we were knocked out by Paris Saint-Germain, we always felt there was a bigger goal to achieve. To do that in the most difficult league in the world in a period of time where it gets harder and harder to win. It is very special. I don't think we are training on Monday!'

Post-match notes

The Reds are crowned Premier League champions — moving 15 points clear of Arsenal with only four games remaining — reaching 20 titles in all.

![L.F.C. crest]

MAY

2025

Not too many points were collected this month but there were plenty of guards of honour and one gleaming trophy at the end of the final game - just what everyone had been hoping for when the season kicked off

Coming up:
4th: Chelsea (PL) A
11th: Arsenal (PL) H
19th: Brighton & Hove Albion (PL) A
25th: Crystal Palace (PL) H

Sunday, May 4th, 4.30pm
Premier League
Chelsea 3 Liverpool 1

Goal: Van Dijk (85)

Line-up (4-2-3-1): Alisson, Alexander-Arnold (Bradley 57), Quansah,
Van Dijk (c), Tsimikas (Chiesa 82), Endo (Mac Allister 69), Jones,
Salah, Elliott (Szoboszlai 69), Gakpo, Jota (Nunez 58).
Subs not used: Kelleher, Diaz, Konate, Robertson

Arne's post-match reaction: 'Nothing good comes from losing
a game of football, but if I have to take the positives, there
were definitely a few positives. Dominating ball possession at
Stamford Bridge is not what many teams do over here because
Chelsea are so comfortable with the ball as well. Being 2-0
down, don't give up; try to fight ourselves back into the game –
and that's what we did. We already had two big chances, which
we didn't score, and then Chelsea were on the counter-attack a
few times [and] very threatening.

Then when we scored for 2-1, I was like, 'Let's see if there's
something in it…' But I don't think there was a moment where
we were close to scoring a goal. In the end, a correct penalty being
given and Chelsea won it 3-1. Maybe [it was] the opposite from
the home game where they dominated possession and we won.
Now it was the opposite.

212

What we also saw today were a lot of things that we've seen throughout the whole season. Us playing through the high press of the opponent so many times and so many moments that we arrived in the final third. But I also saw us defending today, not that I am used to it always, so the last percentages were not of a normal standard. In the final third we come there so many times, and normally we are able to create more chances.

That could mean two things. Either Chelsea did well in both boxes, which they did, but I think it tells us also a little bit about us. In general, [it was] a good performance, but the final percentages weren't there to win this game of football. [In] the lead-up to both goals a player of ours slipped. Would it have happened as well if the game was on the line? Yes or no, we will never know – but the margins are small in the Premier League, especially if you play a team like Chelsea with so many quality players, then you cannot afford these kind of moments.

Yes, we all have quality players. Chelsea have them, [Manchester] City have them, Arsenal have them, [Aston] Villa have them... we have them as well. But the margins are small, and that's why you have to work so hard every three days to get so many points onboard. That's what we did this season.'

Post-match notes

Arne Slot made six changes to the side that had clinched the title against Tottenham in their previous match. It was the Reds' second away defeat of the season.

Arne Slot

v Arsenal
Sunday, May 11th, 4.30pm

'THE SUPPORT, COLOUR, PASSION, NOISE AND JOY THAT OUR SUPPORTERS CREATED IS VERY SPECIAL'

Premier League

Good afternoon and welcome to Anfield for our Premier League fixture against Arsenal.

The first thing for me to say ahead of this match is very straightforward – thank you. Thank you for the unbelievable scenes that followed our last home game, and thank you to those who took the party to Stamford Bridge last week.

The support, colour, passion, noise and joy that our supporters have created over the last two weekends is something that is very special, and in my experience of football so far, it is also unique. In these moments we are reminded why we work as hard as we do and why this club means as much as it does to so many people.

This makes winning together such an incredible experience, and it is one that all of us would like to recreate in the future. But – and I hate to be the person who comes with a "but" in a situation like this – as well as enjoying everything about our achievement, we now have to start climbing the mountain all over again.

I was pleased with many elements of our performance against Chelsea, particularly the way we responded to being behind, but the fact is we lost, and as a wise man once said to me, no good can ever come of losing football games. That defeat gives today's game an extra importance because ever since we were crowned champions, our aim has been to end this season as strongly as we possibly can.

As everyone knows, Arsenal are a very good team,

and along with Manchester City, they were one of the benchmarks for us when I first arrived as head coach last June. That we have managed to finish above them is testament to the hard work and effort that has been put in by everyone at the club, on and off the pitch. Again, though, this is Liverpool Football Club, and our aim should always be to go one better, and today's game gives us an opportunity to do this.

For that to happen we need absolute focus and total motivation. We also need the full Anfield experience because at its best the atmosphere in this stadium will always push our players on. None of this is to say we should not enjoy what we have done this season. It is just that the best way of enjoying it is by being the team, the club, and the supporters that have won the Premier League.

I would like to welcome Mikel Arteta, his players, and the staff and supporters of Arsenal to Anfield for today's game. No-one needs to tell me of Arsenal's quality. They have shown how strong they are in this country over a number of years and have also highlighted it with their run to the Champions League semi-finals this season. Their misfortune in that competition was the same as ours in terms of coming up against an incredibly strong Paris Saint-Germain, although Arsenal at least got to wait until the last four to meet them.

Looking back to the last time we played Arsenal back in October, that was yet another fixture in which the small margins of the Premier League were laid bare. I said at the time we deserved to find ourselves behind at half-time and that made our second-half fightback to get a valuable point hugely satisfying, especially after being away in Europe just a few days earlier.

We were able to get a very good result from a very difficult away game, and even though we are at home today, I do not expect this fixture to be any easier. If we want to get another positive result and if we want to be able to keep on enjoying the end of this season as much as we would like to, the only way to give ourselves the best possible chance is by giving absolutely everything – on and off the pitch.

Liverpool 2 Arsenal 2

Goals: Gakpo (20), Diaz (21)

Line-up (4-2-3-1): Alisson, Bradley (Alexander-Arnold 67), Konate, Van Dijk (c), Robertson, Gravenberch (Elliott 83), Jones (Nunez 67), Salah, Szoboszlai, Gakpo (Mac Allister 66), Diaz (Jota 79). Subs not used: Kelleher, Endo, Quansah, Tsimikas

Arne's post-match reaction: 'I said to everyone that asked me that question [about the reaction to Alexander-Arnold] that it is a privilege to live in Europe, where everybody can have his own opinion. That is something we saw today as well. A few of them were not happy with him [after announcing he was to leave the club]. I think all of them are not happy with him leaving. A few of them booed him. And a few of them clapped.

The only thing I can say about it is that I owe it to the players and to the club and to the staff – for everyone who worked so hard for us to win a game of football – to try to do that. And if we are, after 70 minutes, 2-2 and Conor [Bradley] can't continue and I have a world-class full-back on the bench, I bring him in. And I think it's a big compliment for him because you can understand how mixed the emotions were in his head probably as well; that you bring in a performance like that tells you why I think, why everybody thinks, he is a world-class full-back. Because with him we were quite close to winning this game, and that's what I owe to the players in the dressing room that work so hard every single day: to make decisions to try to win the game.

I think all over this is why people like the Premier League so much: two great teams that are competing with each other and a fantastic game of football. Both teams showing so much quality. Four goals, 2-2; both teams could have won it in the end. This is what makes the Premier League so special and this is also what we have to try as managers, not only to win games but also make sure the fans like what they see.'

Post-match notes

Cody Gakpo's first-half goal against Arsenal saw him become only the second Liverpool player ever to score in 10 consecutive starts at Anfield. Mo Salah (December 2017 to April 2018) was the first.

Monday, May 19th, 8pm
Premier League
Brighton 3 Liverpool 2

Goals: Elliott (9), Szoboszlai (45+1)

Line-up (4-2-3-1): Alisson, Bradley (Endo 77), Konate, Quansah, Tsimikas, Gravenberch, Szoboszlai (Jones 63), Salah (c), Elliott, Gakpo (Diaz 63), Chiesa (Nunez 63). Subs not used: Kelleher, Alexander-Arnold, Gomez, Robertson, Van Dijk

Arne's post-match reaction: 'A great game of football. Two teams that wanted to play, two teams that wanted to win, had no intentions to do things that people normally don't like to see if they watch a game of football, so no time-wasting, no tumbling. Two teams that were just for almost 100 minutes trying to win a game of football, with some brilliant individual moments. I've seen a few from us, but the lead-up to the 2-2, the ball from the goalkeeper towards that midfielder that pretended to play the ball to the outside and then played [to] his midfielder, was a great moment from them, and then the lead-up to the 3-2, the way Mitoma bounced that ball behind his standing leg towards the midfielder that came underneath him. [They] were, from their perspective, great moments, and I think there were many of those moments during the whole game from both sides.

I saw many things that I already knew, and one of them is

how close the margins have been throughout our whole season. And now with us failing to score the third, with us just missing maybe this two or three percent sometimes in our defensive work, immediately it leads to us losing games of football.

But we won this league because we've been so consistent, we've done so many things right, but we haven't won it in a way like [Manchester] City did it for the last four seasons, where they just could close the eyes and they were even 4-0 up. We've been very close in terms of quality with all the teams we've competed with. That's why it's also such a big compliment that we won this league by such a big margin, because the quality margins are not so much different between us and some other teams, so that's why it's such a big compliment.

What I liked a lot is that we mostly have a certain routine in our set-pieces but we tried to tell them, if you see something else, try to execute it. Feel free to execute if you feel there is another opportunity. I think Harvey [Elliott] and Dom [Szoboszlai] felt it was a two-v-one at that free-kick and they outplayed that. Then, I definitely feel Dom meant to shoot that ball on target because he has a great shot, and we ask him, 'Use it more, use it more,' because in training sessions he scores from every angle.'

Post-match notes

Despite losing to Brighton, Liverpool achieved a club first: scoring in every single away league match this campaign.

v Crystal Palace
Sunday, May 25th, 4pm

'THIS IS ONE OF THE BIGGEST DAYS IN THE MODERN HISTORY OF LIVERPOOL FOOTBALL CLUB'

Good afternoon and welcome to Anfield for our final Premier League fixture of the season against Crystal Palace.

I have only been at Liverpool for one year, but I know how much the supporters of this club have waited for this day. Lifting the Premier League trophy in front of fans is something that so many people have longed for and this means it is a privilege for all of us who are fortunate enough to be involved, no matter which role we are in.

For me as head coach, my overriding feeling is pride, but not for myself – for the players, the staff, the supporters, the club, and the city. The hard work and effort, the commitment, and the devotion that has been put in, not just this season but also in the years before, is why we are in the position to make today every bit as special as we all could wish for.

This means it is a day for unity and celebration. Nothing can be allowed to get in the way. Whatever might divide us can wait for another day. Whatever could distract us can be put to one side. This is one of the biggest days in the modern history of Liverpool Football Club, so it makes sense that we all contribute to making it as positive as it can be and enjoy it as much as possible. Again, nothing else matters.

The reason I am saying this is I am as aware as anyone of the situation around Trent, and I know, because these feelings have been made clear, that there are some of you who would prefer for him not to be involved today.

The first thing I have to make clear is that whatever your view, we all want what is best for this club, and it is always so, so important that we all remember this.

For some of our supporters, I know they believe it is not right that a player who has told us he will be leaving us and who will leave us when his contract expires should be given further opportunities to play for us. As I have said from the outset, it is not my place to question how people feel, particularly when they give as much to Liverpool FC as our supporters do.

What I maybe should do more though is explain why as a head coach I see things differently. Firstly, as his manager, I am as disappointed as anyone that Trent is leaving. But also as his manager I have a responsibility to take care of all of my players, even at moments when I am disappointed. This is an essential part of my role at all times.

On top of this, I can only ever appreciate every player who has contributed to what we have achieved this season. The future can and will look after itself, and we will move on as a club, just as Liverpool always has. But in the here and now, every single player who has worn a red shirt this season by being part of this team and helped us become champions can only have my appreciation.

This is why I strongly believe that every player who falls into this category deserves today to be as special as it possibly can be. I have the exact same feelings about our supporters. You deserve this day as much as anyone. Just as against Tottenham on the day we won the league, I want everything to be as close to perfect as possible. This is why I believe differences are for another day.

Of course, before the celebrations can begin, we have another big responsibility, which is to do everything we can – again, together – to produce the kind of performance that a day like this deserves. This, I can say without hesitation, will not be easy. Crystal Palace are a team that has so much quality, but it also has an outstanding team ethic, and we recognised both in our fixture against them at Selhurst Park earlier this season.

The fact that they went on to win the FA Cup last weekend is therefore no surprise whatsoever, but this does not make it any less of a magnificent achievement. Everyone knows of my admiration for Pep Guardiola, and Manchester City's status as one of Europe's strongest teams is not in question, so Palace's victory on the day was truly outstanding.

For this reason, I would like to take this opportunity to congratulate Oliver Glasner, the Palace players, staff, and supporters for winning the FA Cup. We have had a lot of credit ourselves in recent weeks, so it is good to be able to give credit to another team which has achieved success.

As we know well, this is one of the toughest countries, if not the toughest country, to be successful in, so hopefully Palace can enjoy the last day of the season also, but not too much!

For us, as I said at the start, it is about enjoying the moment. After that we get to take a break while continuing to work towards the future. One of the many great things about having success is that it makes you want it more and more, and this is our challenge now. Winning the Premier League is incredible in itself but we can not and will not stop here.

Liverpool 1 Crystal Palace 1

Goal: Salah (84)

Line-up (4-2-3-1): Alisson, Bradley (Alexander-Arnold 46), Konate (Jota 62), Van Dijk, Robertson (Elliott 85), Jones, Gravenberch, Salah, Szoboszlai (Nunez 61), Gakpo, Diaz (Endo 69).
Subs not used: Kelleher, Gomez, Quansah, Tsimikas

Arne's post-match reaction: 'Another special day. Less pressure than four weeks ago, of course, when we had to win the game to get those celebrations. Now we knew we would get them. The energy in the stadium, how loud the fans were, the way the game ended in the last half-hour, going down to 10 men and then seeing such a great reaction from the players and the fans, which led to, in my opinion, a deserved goal — we deserved to go 1-1. These players and these fans hate losing, don't want to lose, and that's what we showed again today.

I think the word 'brilliant' and our fans go together. So, how brilliant they were before the Tottenham game, during the Tottenham game, and afterwards, I don't think you see many special celebrations as you saw four weeks ago. I don't think that you see many of them like we had today. It's no surprise to me at all that they were brilliant again today, as they were throughout the whole season, as they were towards Trent [Alexander-Arnold]. But maybe it also helps what an unbelievable half he played. The passes he played, if you make a highlight of this, probably it's going to take you three, four, or five minutes. The ball to Darwin [Nunez] was another level; it was next level.

He deserved it. I'm very happy for him, for everyone in and around the club that things worked out as they did. I think everybody could see how difficult he had it after the game, and that tells you how hard it is to leave a club like this. That's all we can try to do: to make it so hard for the players to leave. Many of them stay, now Trent has made the decision to go, unfortunately for us. But it was great for him to have a farewell, as he had today.

A few of them have already shown that they can win multiple times. I'm talking about the ones that have won the league and the Champions League here before, and these are also the players that just keep on performing year after year after year, even if they don't win it.

A few of them now won the league for the first time, and they have to show that they have the same mentality as the ones that have won it here before. I'm looking forward to being part of that. We know it's going to be tough again. It was already very tough this season. It's going to be probably just as tough or even tougher next season because the club that we've competed with this season have in every window, always invested a lot of money, and they're probably going to do so this summer as well.

We did things differently last season. I don't think it has been said a lot, but maybe I'm completely wrong because the one that told me maybe lied to me, but he said to me that since Alex Ferguson won the league, the last time he won the league, not a team has had so many academy minutes as our academy players had this season. So that's been really special. Apart from signing Federico Chiesa last summer, we didn't do a lot, and that makes it maybe even more special to win it this season. Now we will see [what] the team needs. We can do things better already by ourselves without adding any players. But if we can, then we will definitely do so.

We just want good players, and ideally you sign them as soon as you can. But it's not always easy to sign good players, let alone to sign them early in the window. But this club doesn't start working from today onwards. There is so much hard work being done behind the scenes already this season to find out which targets we have and try to sign them. I have all the confidence that if we've addressed the right player that we try to sign that player. But let's see when that's going to happen and if that's going to happen because I'm very happy with the squad we already have.

How passionate these fans are for the club and how special it is to win something, let alone over here. I think I could feel today that it was 35 years ago that they were part of it. It's only been five years ago that we won the league, but unfortunately the fans couldn't be there. Now they were, and I think everybody could see what it means for the fans to win it, and that is what makes it special and, in the end, for us as well. Because you play football for yourself, for your family, but definitely also for the fans, and we are privileged that we can play it in front of these [fans] because these ones are special, which they're going to again show tomorrow. Because if other teams or clubs show the trophy in their city, then there are other people there, some great videos you can see – but I think this is again going to be next level.'

Post-match notes

Mohamed Salah crowned a stellar season with his 29th Premier League goal to add to his 18 assists.

A word from some of Slot's title-winners...

Mohamed Salah

'Incredible. Incredible to win the Premier League here with the fans – [it] is something special. You saw that today and you saw it in the game. It's an incredible feeling to win the Premier League here with Liverpool and the fans.

'This is way better [than five years ago], 100 per cent... It feels more special with the fans, but I don't want to take that from anyone. You have a different group now and a different manager. To show you're able to do it again is something special.'

Virgil van Dijk

'It's special and something that we don't take for granted. It's amazing. It's amazing what today was. There was a lot of emotions before the game and all week, but we got the job done. We are truly deserved champions.

'[It's] the most beautiful club in the world and I think [they] deserve all of this. Let's enjoy the next couple of weeks and let it sink in.'

Alisson Becker

'Oh my God, it's difficult to put it in words. But it means a lot. It's a mix of feelings. I was really emotional, to be honest with you; so many things go through your mind. So much sacrifice that we do. So many challenges that we had to face: changing managers, injuries. Myself, I had a big injury this season, the concussion as well. But winning the way we did, in front of the supporters, with the game – an amazing game that we played – this is fantastic. It's amazing, special.'

Curtis Jones

'I'm speechless; it's everything. Plus, I'm a Scouse lad as well, I've come all the way through [the ranks]. I was fortunate enough to have been part of the first one; I didn't play a load of games. But now I feel like I'm a big part of this; I've played more games, I've scored goals, I've assisted, I've helped the team. I'm just taking it all in.'

Ryan Gravenberch

'It was really amazing. From the start we felt, 'Oh, they [the fans] are here' and we wanted to do our stuff for them – and we did it.'

Cody Gakpo

'It's amazing. We worked really hard this year. [We have had] special moments, lesser moments in the Champions League, but to get this is amazing. The Dutch impact – I think you guys saw it already. Virgil [van Dijk] is here already a long time, but this year Ryan [Gravenberch] is playing like how we knew him in Holland; he played [like] that here.

'It's amazing to see him play like this, and obviously the coach tactically brought the whole team to another level and I think that suits the players we have now. Hopefully we can gear up a little more in the next few years, but it's a good start.'

Alexis Mac Allister

'To win a World Cup and now a Premier League is something really special. It's an achievement I really, really enjoyed – but it wouldn't be possible without my teammates. They are the most important thing for me. I am just one part of the puzzle.

'This team is really, really good. It's something really special and hopefully this win, we can enjoy it.'

Andy Robertson

'The last time we won it was a stranger time, but I suppose we kind of got that feeling against Man United at home. It was pretty much done at that point with [being] 16 or 19 points clear. Then obviously the world paused. It was quite unique the way we did it. We enjoyed it, of course we did, but you can't beat how we went to the ground and the fans during and after the game. Nothing quite compares to that, and I'm glad we got to experience it that way as well.'

SEASON STATISTICS

The numbers that illustrate the contribution Arne Slot's players made to a campaign of success

Appearances (all competitions)

Name	PL	FA	LC	Europe	Total
Mohamed Salah	38	0	5	9	52
Luis Diaz	36	1	4	9	50
Cody Gakpo	35	0	6	8	49
Dominik Szoboszlai	36	1	3	9	49
Alexis Mac Allister	35	0	6	8	49
Ryan Gravenberch	37	0	3	9	49
Virgil van Dijk	37	0	3	9	49
Darwin Nunez	30	2	6	9	47
Curtis Jones	33	0	5	8	46
Andy Robertson	33	0	4	8	45
Trent Alexander-Arnold	33	1	2	8	44
Ibrahima Konate	31	0	4	7	42
Diogo Jota	26	2	5	4	37
Alisson Becker	28	0	1	6	35
Wataru Endo	20	2	4	6	32
Kostas Tsimikas	18	2	3	6	29
Conor Bradley	19	1	4	5	29
Harvey Elliott	18	2	3	5	28
Jarell Quansah	13	2	6	4	25
Caoimhin Kelleher	10	2	4	4	20
Joe Gomez	9	1	3	4	17
Federico Chiesa	6	2	3	3	14
Trey Nyoni	0	2	2	1	5
Tyler Morton	0	1	3	1	5
Jayden Danns	1	1	1	1	4
James McConnell	0	2	1	1	4
Vitezslav Jaros	1	0	1	0	2
Isaac Mabaya	0	1	0	0	1
Amara Nallo	0	0	0	1	1
Rio Ngumoha	0	1	0	0	1
Trent Kone-Doherty	0	1	0	0	1

Goals (all competitions)

Name	PL	FA	LC	Europe	Total
Mohamed Salah	29	0	2	3	34
Cody Gakpo	10	0	5	3	18
Luis Diaz	13	0	1	3	17
Diogo Jota	6	1	2	0	9
Dominik Szoboszlai	6	0	1	1	8
Alexis Mac Allister	5	0	0	2	7
Darwin Nunez	5	0	1	1	7
Virgil van Dijk	3	0	1	1	5
Harvey Elliott	1	0	1	3	5
Trent Alexander-Arnold	3	1	0	0	4
Curtis Jones	3	0	0	0	3
Ibrahima Konate	1	0	0	1	2
Federico Chiesa	0	1	1	0	2
Jayden Danns	0	1	0	0	1
Own goals	1	0	0	0	1

All competitions:
Total games: 56
Games won: 38
Clean sheets: 22
Total goals: 123
Average home attendance: 60,210

Player debuts:
Federico Chiesa (v AC Milan 17.09.24)
Vitezslav Jaros (v Crystal Palace 05.10.24)
Rio Ngumoha (v Accrington Stanley 11.01.25)
Amara Nallo (v PSV Eindhoven 29.01.25)
Trent Kone-Doherty (v Plymouth Argyle 09.02.25)
Isaac Mabaya (v Plymouth Argyle 09.02.25)

Season Statistics

Final Premier League table

2024-25 season

	P	W	D	L	F	A	GD	Pts
1 Liverpool (C)	**38**	**25**	**9**	**4**	**86**	**41**	**+45**	**84**
2 Arsenal	38	20	14	4	69	34	+35	74
3 Manchester City	38	21	8	9	72	44	+28	71
4 Chelsea	38	20	9	9	64	43	+21	69
5 Newcastle United	38	20	6	12	68	47	+21	66
6 Aston Villa	38	19	9	10	58	51	+7	66
7 Nottingham Forest	38	19	8	11	58	46	+12	65
8 Brighton & Hove Albion	38	16	13	9	66	59	+7	61
9 Bournemouth	38	15	11	12	58	46	+12	56
10 Brentford	38	16	8	14	66	57	+9	56
11 Fulham	38	15	9	14	54	54	0	54
12 Crystal Palace	38	13	14	11	51	51	0	53
13 Everton	38	11	15	12	42	44	−2	48
14 West Ham United	38	11	10	17	46	62	−16	43
15 Manchester United	38	11	9	18	44	54	−10	42
16 Wolverhampton Wanderers	38	12	6	20	54	69	−15	42
17 Tottenham Hotspur	38	11	5	22	64	65	−1	38
18 Leicester City	38	6	7	25	33	80	−47	25
19 Ipswich Town	38	4	10	24	36	82	−46	22
20 Southampton	38	2	6	30	26	86	−60	12